Table of Contents

Preface

You want what you want.

Invisibility. Anonymity. Ghost protocol.

You've taken the red pill and have seen the truth, and you don't like it. I don't blame you. I didn't like it either. But what I thought I knew about Tor and other incognito tools was only a drop in the ocean next to what's really out there. Stuff you don't find on many tech forums. They're whispered in private, of course, but it's all invisible to you. Until now.

Which brings us to you and I, or rather what I can do for you. It's amazing what a guy can learn in a decade when he rolls his sleeves up and gets his hands dirty. Private hacker forums. Usenet. Freenet. I scoured them all for years and what I've learned isn't anywhere else on Amazon.

Equally amazing is what you can learn for a few dollars in a weekend's worth of reading. That's me, and soon to be *you*. Where you will be by Monday is where I am now, only without the years of mistakes. Mistakes I made using Freenet, Tails, PGP. You name it, I did it. And boy did I make BIG ONES. Those are mistakes you'll avoid because, after you've read this guide, you'll know more than 85% of the Tor users out there, and know more about anonymity than most Federal agents. Even the so-called superhackers at the NSA who only get by with a minimum amount of work every day, mostly involving eradicating your right to privacy.

To that, if you don't come away satisfied, return it for a full refund.

But I know you won't. Because once you've taken the red pill, there ain't no going back. You can't unlearn what you've learned, unsee what you've seen, and you'll want more. Much, much more.

First off, we're not sticking with the basics here. If all you want is Tor for Dummies, look elsewhere. Where we're going is dangerous territory. It's shark territory when you get right down to it. But don't worry. We've got shark repellant and everything you need to surf safe. You'll reap benefits you've only dreamed of and by the time we're done, you'll have gained NSA-level anonymity skills with a counter-surveillance mindset that rivals anything Anonymous or those goons at the NSA can come up with. They won't have a clue as to how to find you.

Secondly, for a few dollars, you'll know every exploit those superhackers like to wield against Tor users and more: How to avoid NSA tracking. Bitcoin anonymity (that is, *real* Bitcoin anonymity), Opsec advice, Darknet markets and Darkcoins and, well... frankly it's a very long list, and by the time you're done you'll be a Darknet *artist* when it comes to marketplaces and buying things cloak and dagger style.

Third, we'll go over many techniques used by the CIA and FBI to entrap users. False confessions. Clickbait. Tor honeypots. It's all the same when you get right down to it. You'll learn the same techniques used to catch terrorists, hackers and rogue members of the hacker group Anonymous and couriers for Reloaded. Baits and lures and how to spot an LEA agent from a mile away. I break it all down into simple steps that you can understand. A few dollars for this info will save you a LIFETIME of grief. And no, you won't find it on Reddit or Ars Technica or Wired. If you're mulling this over, don't. You need this now. Not when you're framed for something you didn't do.

Fourth... reading the dangerous material herein requires you take ACTION. The Feds take action. Identity thieves take action. Hackers take action. Will you? You have to take action if you want results. What you're glossing over right now is no mere guide. It's a *mindset*. It's professional level stuff meant to keep you and your family safe for a decade out, going far beyond apps and proxies and it's all yours if you do two simple things: Read, then act. Simple. Because you know what they say: Knowledge is power.

No, strike that. Knowledge is *potential* power. *Your* power. But only if you act.

Fifth... I update this book every month. New browser exploit in the wild? I update it here. New technique for uncloaking Tor users? You'll read it here first. We all know how Truecrypt is Not Safe Anymore, but that's only the beginning. Besides, freedom isn't free.

Lastly... The scene from Jurassic Park with Dennis Nedry, I believe, is a nice frightful analogy to what happens if you don't take your security seriously. We see poor Dennis try to get his jeep out of the muck in the middle of a tropical storm. Lightning unzips the sky and the rain pours. The thunder rolls. A dilophisaur bounds upon him, beautiful and appearing curious. Yet boiling under his head lies a deadly secretion as it sniffs the air and cocks it's head at Nedry - moments before spraying his chubby eyes with poison. Blinded, he staggers back to the safety of the jeep, wailing and gnashing teeth, only to discover a visual horror to his right: he's left the passenger-side door ajar - wide enough to let Mr. Curious in for a juicy evening meal, which it savors with a row of piranha-sharp teeth.

The point is this: Don't be Dennis Nedry. There are far bigger creatures who'd like nothing better than to split your life (and family) wide open if for no other reason because THEY CAN. Such is the nature of the elite.

Unless, of course, you tame them...

Which is not bloody likely.

Is Tor Safe?

That seems to be the question alright. As to what the true answer is, it really depends on whom you ask, because there are always wolves in sheep's clothing out there who stand to gain from your ignorance. Many say no. A few say yes. The media, for all their expertise in things political and social, come up woefully lacking when something as complex as Tor is discussed.

Case in point: Gizmodo reported that in December, 2014, a group of hackers managed to compromise enough Tor relays to decloak Tor users. If you're just hearing this for the first time, part of what makes Tor anonymous is that it relays your data from one node to another. It was believed that if they compromised enough of them, then they could track individual users on the Tor network and reveal their real life identities. Kind of like how the agents in The Matrix find those who've been unplugged.

Anyway as luck would have it, it turned out to be kiddie script-hackers with too much time on their hands who simply wanted a new target to hack. Who knows why. Could be that they'd toyed with the Playstation Network long enough and simply wanted a curious peak here and there. These were not superhacker-level NSA members, either.

But as is usually the case with the media, this attack attracted the attention of a few bloggers and tech journalists unsympathetic to Tor and frankly, ignorant of what really constitutes a threat. The Tor devs commented on it, too:

"This looks like a regular attempt at a Sybil attack: the attackers have signed up many new relays in hopes of becoming a large fraction of the network. But even though they are running thousands of new relays, their relays currently make up less than 1% of

the Tor network by capacity. We are working now to remove these relays from the network before they become a threat, and we don't expect any anonymity or performance effects based on what we've seen so far."

What those conspiracy bloggers failed to report was that any decentralized network like Tor is a prime target for attacks such as the above. But to truly stand a chance at punching a hole through this matrix, hackers would need Tor to implicitly trust every new node that comes online. That just doesn't happen.

It also takes time for fresh relays to gather traffic - some as long as sixty days or more and the *likelihood* of being reported is rather high since the IP addresses are out in the open, which only speeds up malicious reporting. The *real* danger, and has been since inception, is scaring Tor users to less secure methods of communication. That's what the NSA wants. The CIA already does this in foreign countries. Now the NSA is following their lead.

The REAL Risk of Using Tor

I list them here before we dive deep into enemy territory so you'll know what to avoid before installation, and maybe get an "a-ha!" moment in subsequent chapters. As you read, remember that having Javascript on is really only a drop in the ocean next to what is possible for an enemy to kill your anonymity.

Javascript

It's widely known that leaving Javascript on is bad for a Tor user. Ninety-five percent of us know this, but the mistakes of the 5% get blown out of proportion and thrown into the face of the rest of us. Worse, many websites now run so many scripts that it seems as though they hate Tor users.

One site required over a dozen. Without it, the page was/is/will be pretty much gimped. Sometimes it's not even *readable*. You can imagine what might happen if you were using Tor and decided to visit that site if it were created to lure users into a honeypot. I recall one researcher claimed that "81% of Tor users can be de-anonymised."

Bull.

That 81% figure came about because the targeted users knew little about the NoScript browser add-on, and likely mixed Tor usage with their daily open net usage, providing ample data for a correlation attack. But that was just the icing on the cake. They left personal details *everywhere*; using the same usernames and passes they do elsewhere on the open net. Bragging about their favorite Netflix movies. Talking about local events (Jazzfest in New Orleans!). The weather (Hurricane in the French Quarter!). You get the idea. Much more on this later.

Volunteering as an Exit Node

Another doozy, though not quite the granddaddy of all risks. It's still risky. On the plus side, you as a valiant believer in anonymity graciously provide bandwidth and an "exit pipe" to the rest of the Tor users (hopefully none of whom you know) so that they may pass their encrypted traffic through your node. Generous? Certainly. Wise? If you live in the States... hale no, as my Uncle Frick in Texas used to say.

It isn't that it is illegal *per se* to do so. On the contrary, but what passes through your Tor node can land you in hot water if you live in a police state like my native Louisiana. All exiting traffic from your node (i.e. *other people's traffic*) is tied to your IP address, and as others have found, you put yourself at risk by what others on the other side of the planet do with your node.

Lots of new Tor users fire up BitTorrent that's been configured for Tor and suck down all the bandwidth. It makes for a very miserable Tor experience for other users. You may get served with a copyright violation notice (or sued), or perhaps even raided at 6 AM by a black party van if child porn ends up flowing out of your pipes. Think carefully and do your research before taking on such a risky charge, lest your computer be seized and your reputation ruined. Innocent men have gone to jail for their overconfidence. (see: https://www.torproject.org/eff/tor-legal-faq.html.en)

Running an Exit Relay From Home

Running it from home is even worse then using cloud storage, and is infinitely more dangerous in the USA and UK than say, Thailand or Philippines. If the law for whatever reason has an interest in your Tor traffic, your PC may just be seized, yes, but that's only the start. In the UK, there are no 5th amendment protections against self-incrimination. Anywhere. A crusty old judge can give you two years just for not forking over the encryption keys. If they did have it, they wouldn't have bothered raiding your bedroom and spooking the bejeezus out of your cat at the crack of dawn.

Use a host instead that supports Tor. There is Sealandhosting.org, for one. They accept Bitcoins and don't require any personal info. Only an email. They offer Socks, Dedicated Servers, Tor Hosting and VPS as well as Domains.

We'll get into the nitty details later, but these are the Rules I've set for myself on occasion. I change them every year.

- Refrain from routing normal traffic through it

- Never do anything illegal (more on this later as it's a very grey area)

- Never put sensitive files on it (for ex., financial data, love notes, court documents, lawyer correspondence)

- Be as transparent as possible that I'm running a Tor exit.

- If I get complaints from ISP or possibly the university, I use this template at the following link: https://www.torproject.org/eff/tor-dmca-response.html.en

Intelligence Agencies

They've declared war on Tor and its stealth capability. No doubt about it. And though they'll fight tooth and nail to convince you it's for your own good, really what it all comes down to isn't so much national security as it is national **control**: Control over you in that they can't see what you're doing on Tor. Nor do they know why. They don't like that.

It's pomposity on a galactic scale unheard of when you look at how much data they're siphoning from everyone's pipes. Every time some new revelation leaks out of Edward Snowden's mouth regarding the NSA, I think of the Gyro Captain from the Road Warrior film with Mel Gibson; the gangliest, sorriest excuse for a desert raider this side of the Fallout games (who's also frustratingly loveable).

Our loveable sky-raider tries to rob Mel of the gasoline that fuels his souped up Falcon Coupe V8. Only it doesn't end well for him. In the attempt, the poor sod makes himself a slave, a delicious reverse slavery pact that ends up with him carrying Mel's gasoline cans across the desert and Mel's dog nipping at his filthy heels as he begs Mel not to ice him right there and then. In fact if it'd not been for the mercy Mel kindly bestowed, his theft quite literally would have blown up in his face due to the custom bomb underneath the hood. Such a nice guy.

Well. The time for playing nice guy to the NSA is over. They spend so much money and waste so much time chasing you simply because they don't like you or your actions not being **easily identifiable**.

As you probably know, it's more costly to go after a high-value target. But they don't know if you are a high-value target or merely low-hanging fruit. As we've seen in the case of bored Harvard students, anyone can get into serious trouble if they go into Tor blind as a bat.

Even Eric Holder has publicly pointed out that Tor users are "non-US persons" until identified as citizens. It's beyond pompous. It's criminal and unconstitutional and like something scaly that mutated in the desert after an atomic bomb went off. In fact, it almost sounds as if they view ALL Tor users as high-value targets. And by the time you are identified as such, they have acquired enough power to strip you as well as millions of other citizens of their rights to privacy and protection under the Fourth Amendment of the Constitution. They do this using two methods:

The Quantum and FoxAcid System

More on how to defeat this later, but here is the gist of it:

- Both systems depend on secret arrangements made with telcos.

- Both involve lulling the user into a false sense of security.

- Neither system can make changes to a LiveCD (Tails) (that's in our favor)

- Both can be defeated by adhering to consistent security habits.

Defeating this requires a mindset of diligence, and as you probably know, diligence is not compatible with procrastination. Therefore, you must resist the urge to procrastinate.

I say again. DO NOT procrastinate. Decide ahead of time to avoid risky behavior. We'll get to them all. A good, security mindset takes time and effort and commitment to develop, true enough, but should be nurtured from the very beginning, which is why the RISKS are placed up front, ahead of even the installation chapter. Things tend to drag in the middle of a book like this, and are often forgotten.

Speaking of risk, if you want to know what truly keeps me up at night, it's this question:

What do other nations tell high-level CEOs and intelligence agencies (Hong Kong, for instance)?

If the only thing I can trust is my dusty old 486 in my attic with Ultima 7 still installed atop my 28.8k dialup modem, then it's safe to assume *every* commercial entity is jeopardized by the NSA. And if that's true, if the NSA has to jump hoops to spy on us, how easy is it to infiltrate American-owned systems *overseas with our data on those systems*?

If no corporation can keep their private info under wraps, then eventually the endgame may evolve into a Skynet grid similar to the Soviet-era East/West block in which CEOs have to choose east or west. But that's like trying to decide whether you want to be eaten by a grizzly bear or a lion.

That's jumping the gun a bit, but at least now you know the real risks. The main ones, anyway.

Every one of these risks can be minimized or outright defeated using knowledge that is in this book. The sad part is that most readers will forget roughly 80% of what they read. Those who take action will retain that 80% because they are making what they've read a **reality**: Making brilliant chesslike countermoves when the NSA threatens your Queen. If you don't take action, but merely sit there waiting forever to make your move, you forfeit the game. They win. So don't be like a frog in a slowly boiling pot of water, because not only will *you* perish, but your future generations will as well.

Alright then. Enough about the risks. Let's get to it.

Tor Step-by-Step Guide

Now let's answer *what Tor is* and *what it does* and *what it cannot do.* You've no doubt guessed by now it's some kind of hacker's tool, and you'd be half right, but only from the perspective that a powerful tool like Tor can be used for just about anything. In fact anything can be bought (except maybe voluptuous blondes in red dresses) anonymously, as long as you're *cautious* in using it. Tor users who get cocky often get caught doing something illegal. Like insulting the king of Thailand or threatening the President of the USA with a pie to the face.

Before you criticize Tor, try to remember that it's not about buying drugs or porn or exotic white tiger cubs. It's about anonymous communication and privacy - with the main function being that it grants you anonymity by routing your browsing session from one Tor relay to another, in essence masking your IP address such that websites cannot know your real location. This gives the average pc user enormous power to act anonymously online.

This power allows you to:

- Access blocked websites (Facebook if you are in China)
- Access .onion sites that are unreachable via the open internet
- Threaten the president with a pie-to-the-face...and no Secret Service visit!

It does all of this by a process called **onion routing**.

What's onion routing, you ask?

Think of it as a multi-point-to-point proxy matrix. Unlike peer to peer applications like BitTorrent or eMule which expose your IP to everyone, Tor uses a series of intermediary nodes (and thus, IP addresses) that encrypt your data all along the network chain. At the endpoint, your data is decrypted by an exit node so that no one can pinpoint your location or tell which file came from which computer. Due to this anonymizing process, you are anonymous on account of the packed "onion layers" that hide your true IP address. Hence the onion symbol of Tor.

It's even possible to build a site such that only Tor users can access it. Also called "Onion Sites," though technically challenging, you don't need a Ph.D in computer science to build one, or even a Bachelor's degree. You don't need to know how to code at all, in fact, and these Onion sites are unaccessible by anyone using the regular web and regular, non-Torified Firefox.

We'll delve deeper into that later, as well as how to construct a fortress of doom that nothing, not even the NSA, can penetrate.

Installation

Installing Tor is dirt simple. You can download it TorProject.org.

If your ISP blocks you from the Tor site, do this:

- Shoot an email to the Tor developers on their homepage. Tell them the situation. You can get an automated message sent back to you with the Tor installation package attached. That's the simple way.

- The harder way is to use Google. At the main page, do a search for any cached websites, including Tor, that might have the install package to download. Many tech sites may just have it cached on their servers in the event of all-out nuclear war. It's a 50/50 chance but I've found it useful for finding 'discontinued' or blocked applications.

- Get a friend to email you the Tor installation. Ask for Tails, too. Think of Tor as the nuclear weapon and

Tails as the uranium that makes that pretty mushroom cloud in the sky. You don't need both, but it's always better to go the Tails route.

- VERIFY the signature if you obtain it elsewhere other than from the main Tor site, but for the love of all that is sacred and holy Threepwood, **verify** it even if your friend hand-delivers it. I've gotten viruses in the past from friend's sharing what they thought were "clean" apps. Believe me, in a situation where you fire up Tor to discuss nuclear launch codes, you don't want a keylogger mucking things up for you.

Now then. Choose Windows, Linux or the Mac version and know that your default Firefox install won't be overwritten unless you want it to. Both use Firefox, but Tor is a completely separate deal. You'll notice it has the same functions as Firefox: Tabs. Bookmarks. Search box. Menus. It's all here... except your favorite add-ons.

On that point, you might be tempted to install your favorite apps. Don't give in to that temptation. Multiple add-ons that do nothing for your anonymity might assist someone in locating you over Tor by what is known as "Browser fingerprinting."

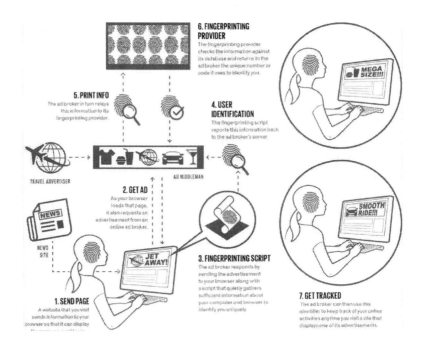

6. FINGERPRINTING PROVIDER
The fingerprinting provider checks the information against its database and returns to the ad broker the unique number or code it uses to identify you.

5. PRINT INFO
The ad broker in turn relays this information to its fingerprinting provider.

4. USER IDENTIFICATION
The fingerprinting script reports this information back to the ad broker's server.

MEGA SIZE!!!

TRAVEL ADVERTISER

AD MIDDLEMAN

2. GET AD
As your browser loads that page, it also requests an advertisement from an online ad broker.

SMOOTH RIDE!!!

NEWS SITE

JET AWAY!

3. FINGERPRINTING SCRIPT
The ad broker responds by sending the advertisement to your browser along with a script that quietly gathers sufficient information about your computer and browser to identify you uniquely.

7. GET TRACKED
The ad broker can then use this identifier to keep track of your online activities anytime you visit a site that displays one of its advertisements.

1. SEND PAGE
A website that you visit sends information to your browser so that it can display

After installation, you should see the green welcome screen below:

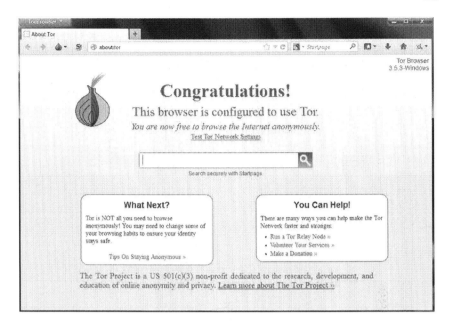

Now you've got some choices. One is to volunteer your bandwidth, which makes it easier for other Tor users, but comes with risk. It's explained in-depth by Tor developers on the TorProject page under the section on relays. I'd recommend reading it if you're new to anonymity tools.

After Tor is installed, every page you visit with the Tor Browser will be routed anonymously through the Tor network. There is, however, an important detail you need to know concerning security, and that is that your Tor settings are merely reasonable **starting points**. They are not optimal, and certainly not bulletproof. We're still at the infancy stage and quite frankly, optimal as Tor knows optimal is largely dependent on hardware (network, CPU, RAM, VM, VPN), and so each person's setup will be different just as a person's security needs in Tehran, Iran are different than in Montreal, Canada.

What Tor Cannot Do

Now for what Tor *cannot* do, or at least cannot do very well. In the future this may change, so don't fall on your sword just yet.

1.) Tor cannot protect you from attachments.

This isn't limited to executables, but anything that can be run by code. This means Flash videos as well as RealPlayer and Quicktime. Those babies can be configured to send your real IP address to an adversary. That's not good. So we must never run any executable or app unless we trust the source implicitly. If at all possible, go *open-source*. This also goes for any encryption scheme. Let's stop right there for a moment.

If you're going to use Tor, encryption is mandatory. It's not an option. I've heard some say on a few encryption blogs that it is, but that's like saying learning Thai is optional if you're going to live in Bangkok all year. You won't get far that way.

2.) Tor cannot run torrents well.

Old news, right? Thousands still do this, and I can understand why with how lawsuit-obsessed North America seems these days. Better safe than sorry, they claim. I've heard every excuse under the rainbow that using torrents on Tor is no big deal. The only problem is... they are safe and **everyone else** is sorry. Tor cannot do P2P apps like Emule and Limewire without making everyone else's Tor experience miserable. It simply sucks down too much bandwidth. In addition to some exit nodes blocking such traffic by default, it's been proven that an IP address can be found by using torrents over Tor. eMule, too, uses UDP and since Tor supports TCP protocol, you can draw your own conclusions about what that does to your anonymity.

True, you may be spared a copyright lawsuit since the RIAA likely won't go through all that trouble in trying to get your IP, but please spare other Tor users the madness of 1998 modem speeds. A VPN is a much better choice, and there are quite a few good ones out there. Visit torrentfreak and key in the search box "Which VPN services take your anonymity seriously." I guarantee you won't be disappointed.

3.) Tor cannot cloak your identity if you neglect Tor - If you're tossing your real email around like Mardi Gras beads, or even if you give your true email on websites while using Tor, you should consider your anonymity compromised. Nuked. Eviscerated. Your virtual identity must never match up with your real-life identity under any circumstance. We'll delve far more deeply in later chapters on how to do this the right way, but know that those who ignore this rule get hacked, robbed, arrested, or mauled by capped gremlins with the letters 'FBI' on their jackets. Much more on this later.

Tor Apps & Anti-Fingerprinting Tools

A few applications, mobile and otherwise, make Tor less of a headache, but they're not particularly well suited for desktop users unless you're doing some kind of emulation. But with everyone using mobile these days, some of these have benefited me in ways I never thought possible. Be sure and read the comments in the Play Store since updates tend to break things.

Orbot: Proxy with Tor

This one is basically Tor for Android, which you can get at the Google Play store or at their homepage.

It is a proxy app that runs similar to the desktop app and encrypts your net traffic, as well as protects you from surveillance and fortifies you against traffic analysis. You can use Orbot with Twitter, DuckDuckGo or any app with a proxy feature. I've used this for a long time now and have gotten used to it's strengths

Invizbox - Privacy Made Easy

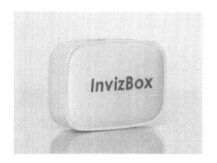

Invizbox plugs into your existing router or modem. A new "InvizBox" WiFi hotspot will appear. Connect to the new hotspot and follow the one time configuration set up and you're ready to go. All devices that you connect to the InvizBox WiFi will route their traffic over the Tor Network. This isn't a required app, mind you, but it makes for simplifying things.

Text Secure

This app encrypts every message on your mobile phone and is simple to learn. Better still, in the event you leave your phone at Marble Slab, rest assured your privacy is safe due to the encryption within. It's also open-source. To that, far too many applications aren't and thus cannot be peer-reviewed by anyone.

Red Phone

One of the more popular apps, this one secures every call with end-to-end encryption, allowing you privacy and peace of mind. It uses WiFi and offers nice upgrades if both callers have RedPhone installed.

It's not for everyone, though. Though it's not as expensive as say, TrustCall, there are convenience issues like lengthy connection times and dropped calls. I experienced a few headaches using Skype to call someone from Manila, so it's not as fast as Jason Bourne's method in all of his movies.

But the pluses outweigh the minuses. I especially love the two-word passphrase as a security feature: If you fear Agent Boris is dead and has been killed by Agent Doris (who now has his phone), you can request she speak the second passphrase. Simple yet effective.

Google and Tor

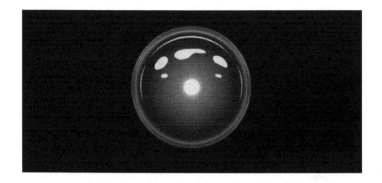

What does Google think of Tor? Quite honestly, I suspect they try not to. In all probability, they probably don't *hate* it like the NSA does, but they know that if every Google user used Tor on a daily basis, much of their ad targeting system would begin firing *blanks*. Imagine if a thirteen year old boy received ads for Cialis, or an eighty-year old woman named Bertha began to see ads for Trojan coupons. It makes for a lousy targeting system. That's good for us. Not so much for Google.

They don't mind donating funds, either, since this allows a future stake in the technology. To that, they've not only donated to Tor, but to other anonymity services too, like Freenet. They've even donated to Mars rover technology. All kinds of outer space things. They never know which technology is going to rocket into orbit a week or year from now, so they throw money around like Scrooge on Christmas morning.

Captchas

At times you'll be using Tor and find that Google spits this requirement out in order to prove you're human. This, on account of their massive analyses on search queries, is what drives some Tor users to think Google has it out for them.

However, Google has to put up with **lots** of spammers and general thievery; bots hammering the servers with tons of queries in short amounts of time that, when added up, puts a huge strain on the servers. It can be just one thing, but it can also happen if your employer uses proxies. For instance, many employees working for the same company that uses one of these can set off a red flag. When your Tor circuit switches to a new one, though, usually it solves itself. There are other search engines like DuckDuckGo you can use, however, if Google is giving you headaches.

And you may find websites do the same thing. Again, this is on account of so many exit nodes, all of which are publicly visible to any website administrator. Slamming the website with such traffic often mimic those of a spambot, the kind Russian and Chinese outfits like to use.

SpiderOak

Normally I warn against using Cloud Service for anything you want private. SpiderOak is one exception I can vouch for, with some reservations. It's a decent enough alternative to DropBox as it's coded with "Zero Knowledge" (so say the developer) and when you install it, a set of encryption keys is created, client-side. When you upload data to SpiderOak servers, they're encrypted on *your* computer and *then* uploaded. Again, according to the developers.

They claim that even if a subpoena requires subscriber data, they could not deliver it since only you have the keys. That sounds very secure, but I still wouldn't upload anything unencrypted that might pique Edward Snowden's curiosity. If it pique's his mind, it'll pique other, more powerful types. Encrypted container files fall into this category.

The other downside is that it's centralized. Centralization means a single-point-of-failure. As well, your data can be deleted by them at any time (true with any online service really). Remember that between you and a judge, they will always side with the judge.

Tails

Ever heard of a "live system"? Neither had I until Tails burst on the scene in 2009. Tails allows you to use Tor to avoid tracking and censorship, and in just about any location you could want. It houses its own operating system, the best part being that it's designed for those on the go.

You can run it via USB stick, SD or even a DVD. This comes pretty handy as it makes it resistant to viruses. It's also beneficial if you don't want your hard drive to leave remnants of your browsing session. The best part is that it's free. Most things based on Linux are, but Tails comes with chat client, email, office, and browser.

The downside to using a DVD though, is that you must burn it again each time you update Tails. That's the inconvenient part. So let's install it to USB stick instead.

1.) Download the Tails installer from the Tails website at tails.boum.org. You must first install it somewhere, like a DVD, and **THEN** clone it the USB stick or SD card.

2.) Click Applications --> Tails --> and then on 'Tails Install' to begin the installation.

3.) Choose Clone & Install to install to SD card or USB Memory Stick

4.) Plug in your device, then scan for the device in the Target-Device drop down menu. You'll get a warning about it overwriting anything on the device. That's nothing to worry about, so choose yes and confirm the install.

Tails Limitations

Neither Tails nor Tor encrypt your documents automatically. You must use GnuPG or LUKS for that, bearing in mind that some documents like Word or Atlantis may have your registration info **within** the document itself. This can be a problem for anonymity. Case in point: in 2013, Amazon self-publishers discovered that pen names could sometimes be revealed by looking at the code of certain word documents and siphoning out the registration information. This code revealed the real identity and addresses of many self-published authors. As an author myself, trust me when I say you don't want the headaches that come with that.

Personally I enter in fake information whenever I "register" any app. All the more so if I will use that app in conjunction with Tor or Tails.

There's other noteworthy stuff to know if you're aim is true anonymity.

Namely:

- Document metadata is not wiped with Tails.
- Tails doesn't hide the fact that you're using it from your ISP (unless you use Tor bridges). They cannot see what you're doing on Tor, true enough, but they know you're using it. Again, unless you use a Tor Bridge.
- Tails is also blind to human error. Try not to use the same Tails session to begin two different projects. Use separate sessions. Isolating both identities in this way contributes to strong anonymity for your sessions.

Chrome

Using Tor with Firefox is hardly the only way to slay a dragon. There's also Chrome. Yes, it's Google, and yes, Google has strayed far from it's "Do No Evil" motto, but like everything else in life, luck favors the prepared and you'd be surprised at how much you can lock down your browser from invaders. Preparations are everything. You just have to have the right sword. The right armor. The right lockpicks. The preparations (reagents) are as follows:

I. Install the ScriptNo extension. It is to chrome what a mouse is for a PC, at least as far as precision goes. It offers excellent control, even allowing you to fine-tune the browser in ways that NoScript for Firefox cannot. If you find it too difficult, ScriptSafe is another option. I've used both and came away very satisfied, though like everything else on the internet, your mileage may vary.

II. FlashControl is a nice alternative to Firefox. In the event you don't see it in the Google Play Store, just search for "Flash Block" and it should come up (Google has a habit of removing apps that aren't updated every Thursday under a Full Moon).

III. Adblock. This one is just insanely good at repelling all kinds of malware. It's probably the most well-known too, so there's plenty of feedback scattered across the internet.

IV. User-agent Switcher for Chrome. Install it. Never leave home (0.0.0.0) without it. It spoofs and mimics user-agent strings. You can set yours to look like Internet Explorer and this will fool a lot of malware payloads into thinking you're really browsing with Internet Explorer and not Firefox or Chrome, thus firing blanks at you.

It might have saved Blake Benthall, 26 year old operator of Silk Road 2.0, from getting raided by the FBI. This was accomplished over the span of many months since they had to get control of many Tor relays, and if you have *control of relays*, you can use sophisticated traffic analysis to study patterns in IP addresses *and* match behavior and browser settings with those addresses. Recall that any federal prosecutor will always try to tie an IP address to an actual person, at least where felonies are concerned.

Let me repeat: An IP address can be considered an *identity* for the purposes of prosecution. It really matters little if you're badmouthing the king of Thailand or inciting a revolution in Tehran or flipping off the Vice President. We're all a number to them for their own agendas.

Those of you with student loans know this perhaps more than anyone else. This will change as time goes on of course, as Tor competitors like Freenet and other apps evolve to offer what Tor cannot. Suffice to say the FBI did their homework and when all was said and done, had more resources on identifying lazy users than a typical VPN would.

V. <u>CanvasBlocker</u> - *Annnnd* another great plugin for Firefox. This baby prevents sites from using Javascript <canvas> API to fingerprint users. You can block it on every site or be discriminant and block only a few sites. It's up to you. The biggest thing for me is that it doesn't *break* websites. More info can be found at <u>browserleaks.com</u> but in case you can't be bothered, here's the gist:

The different block modes are:
</canvas></canvas></canvas>

- block readout API: All websites not on the white list or black list can use the <canvas> API to display something on the page, but the readout API is not allowed to return values to the website.
- fake readout API: Canvas Blocker's default setting, and my favorite! All websites not on the white list or black list can use the <canvas> API to display something on the page, but the readout API is forced to return a new random value each time it is called.

- ask for readout API permission: All websites not on the white list or black list can use the <canvas> API to display something on the page, but the user will be asked if the website should be allowed to use the readout API each time it is called.

- block everything: Ignore all lists and block the <canvas> API on all websites.

- allow only white list: Only websites in the white list are allowed to use the <canvas> API.

- ask for permission: If a website is not listed on the white list or black list, the user will be asked if the website should be allowed to use the <canvas> API each time it is called.

- block only black list: Block the <canvas> API only for websites on the black list.

- allow everything: Ignore all lists and allow the <canvas> API on all websites.

As you can see, it's powerful stuff.

Deadly Firefox Options

Firefox

You might be tempted to enable "Check for counterfeit websites" in Firefox. Don't do this, as it will relay sites you regularly visit to Google's servers. Google's "predictive text-search" is also bad as it relays keystrokes to Google as well. To change it you have to do it manually by going into about:config in the Firefox address bar.

Now let's look at some other privacy settings you might want to know about.

Javascript - This one you should avoid like the black plague, as using it on the Tor network is equivalent to drinking from a well contaminated by the plague in the year 1350. You may notice it is turned on by default under the Firefox options tab, though. The reason is spelled out by the Tor Developer Team:

We configure NoScript to allow JavaScript by default in Tor Browser because many websites will not work with JavaScript disabled. Most users would give up on Tor entirely if a website they want to use requires JavaScript, because they would not know how to allow a website to use JavaScript (or that enabling JavaScript might make a website work).

There's a tradeoff here. On the one hand, we should leave JavaScript enabled by default so websites work the way users expect. On the other hand, we should disable JavaScript by default to better protect against browser vulnerabilities (not just a theoretical concern!). But there's a third issue: websites can easily determine whether you have allowed JavaScript for them, and if you disable JavaScript by default but then allow a few websites to run scripts (the way most people use NoScript), then your choice of whitelisted websites acts as a sort of cookie that makes you recognizable (and distinguishable), thus harming your anonymity.

Ghostery and Ghostrank - These aren't particularly deadly, just useless on Tor since Tor disables tracking anyway. If you do decide to use it, know that using either can alter your browser 'fingerprint' - though not to the extent of breaking anonymity. Ghostery still blocks any tracking scripts regardless if you're on Tor or not. But use DuckDuckGo if you want to beef up your anonymity.

Adblock - We mentioned this one before and, sadly, using this could also change your browser fingerprint. Adblock plus has "acceptable ads" enabled by default, and there is also the scandals that Adblock has been in over the years, one implying that Google paid the Adblock CEO for Google Ads to be shown. You can draw your own conclusions about that, but with so many users applying pressure, you can rest assured that you're not just a number to them anymore.

Besides that, the basic idea of the Tor Browser Bundle is to use as few addons as possible. They figure that TorButton, NoScript, and HTTPS Everywhere is sufficient to preserve anonymity without the added risk of additional addons. Or drama. Along this line of thought, the Panopticlick website may also be useful to you.

Whonix & Tor

If you're paranoid that using Tor could get you into trouble, such as if you host a Hidden Service, you may want to look into Whonix before running anything further. Many power users who use Tor on a daily basis like the tighter security it offers. This isn't to say that it's *better* than Tails by default. Both tools offer their own strengths and weaknesses, and each strength is meant for a different purpose. You may find one is better than the other for *your personal situation*, where the situation differs according to your security needs.

Like Tails, Whonix is built with anonymity *and* security in mind. It's also based off of Debian/Linux, so it's a good synergy where anonymity is concerned. This synergy grants anonymity by routing everything through Tor. The advantages are that DNS leaks are next to impossible and malware cannot reveal your IP address. In fact, the only connections possible are routed through Tor via the Whonix-Gateway.

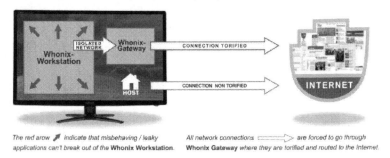

Whonix
Anonymous Operating System

*The red arow ⚡ indicate that misbehaving / leaky applications can't break out of the **Whonix Workstation**.*   *All network connections ┅┅┅> are forced to go through **Whonix Gateway** where they are torified and routed to the Internet.*

The question you may be wondering is: how much security is too much security? What's overkill and what isn't?

Well, the perfect answer to that is this: How far will you fall if caught, and how much time are you willing to invest in reading to prevent it? Tails is easier to grasp, and if you don't expect attacks from sites you visit, then by all means use Tails.

If, however, you live in North Korea or China, then there's the possibility of twenty years of hard labor - hammering worthless rocks. That is, if they see any

Tor activity coming from your location that correlates to "things they don't like" activity... or anything else in the case of North Korea. They don't like it when outsiders offer the peasants hope. If you're caught in that country, you'll be found guilty long before you ever see a judge.

So if the above applies to you, use Whonix.

From Whonix.org:

Security [edit]
Network [edit]

	Whonix	Tails	Tor Browser	Qubes OS TorVM	corridor
Responsible for building Tor circuits	Tor client running on Whonix-Gateway	Tor client running on workstation	Tor client running on workstation	Tor client running on TorVM (Gateway)	Tor client running behind corridor-Gateway
Protection against IP/location discovery [20] on the Workstation. [21]	Yes [22]	No [23]	No [24]	Yes	No [25]
IP/DNS protocol leak protection	Full [25]	Depends [26]	Depends [26]	Full	Depends
Workstation does not have to trust Gateway	No	Not a gateway	Not a gateway	No	Yes
Takes advantage of *Entry Guards* [27]	Yes	No	Yes	Yes	Not applicable [28]

A few notable features of Whonix that make it more secure:

Anonymous Publishing/Anti-Censorship

Anonymous E-Mail w/Thunderbird or TorBirdy

Add proxy behind Tor (user -> Tor -> proxy)

Chat anonymously.

IP/DNS protocol leak protection.

Hide that you are using Tor

Hide the fact you are using Whonix

Mixmaster over Tor

Secure And Distributed Time Synchronization
Mechanism

Security by Isolation

Send E-mail anonymously without registration

Torify any app

Torify Windows

Virtual Machine Images (VM)

VPN Support

Use Adobe Flash anonymously

Use Java/Javascript anonymously

The following is an example of a moderately
secure system:

- Host Whonix on a memory stick with a flavor of Linux of your choice

- Use a <u>VPN</u> you trust. Visit TorrentFreak.com for the 2015 list.

- Use Macchanger to spoof any mac address for every session. But know that Whonix doesn't hide your mac address from sites you visit. If Macchanger isn't to your liking, give Technitium MAC Address Changer a try.

Two other things to note where security is concerned:

- Avoid regular calls of non-Tor WiFi tablets if you're using Cafe WiFi

- Know as well where every CCTV is located in the area you plan to use Tor

<u>MAC Addresses</u>

We mentioned Mac addresses. As technology would have it, your new WiFi/Ethernet card has something that can aid intelligence agencies in tracking you. It's a 48-bit identifier burned-in by the manufacturer. Sort of like an IMEI for your phone. If by chance you weren't thinking clearly and bought your computer with Tor in mind using a credit card, you may later get targeted by an FBI "NIT" that swipes your MAC number. A Nit is short for 'Network Investigative Technique'. If that happens, you're toast, as you'll be tracked by some lackey working for them with far too much time on his hands.

The way to defeat this is to have a disposable MAC address (the number, not the Apple product) - one that you bought with cash with no security cams looking over your shoulder. That way you can get rid of it in a flash or swap it out if you realize they're onto you.

They're also soft-configurable and, believe it or not, Tails itself alters this randomly with every session. With a virtual machine, the FBI Nit may target a MAC number from the VirtualBox pool. This isn't really an issue unless they happen to raid your house and grab your system simultaneously. So swapping this out on a daily basis, as you've probably guessed, can be quite a pain. It's mainly for guys who run illegal markets on the Deep Web. Guys who are *always* in the crosshairs of alphabet agencies.

But then, so can you. I've found it pays to think of oneself higher than what one is actually worth when traversing dark nets. In other words, thinking of yourself as a **high value target**. You'll subconsciously program yourself to research more, learn more - everything from bad security mistakes to bad friendships to bad business practices. To that, you don't have to be in the top 5% of guys who've mastered network security. Being in the top 25% pool is more than enough to make The Man get frustrated enough to look for his flashy headlines elsewhere... like a low hanging fruit named Nasty Neb who lives in his mother's basement, for instance.

Whonix Bridges

If you live in a communist hellscape where even mentioning Tor can get you into trouble, using a Bridge with Whonix can be quite literally a life saver.

What Bridges Are

Bridges are obfuscation tools used to cloak your Tor usage from a nosy ISP or government who might see you're using Tor, but not know what you are doing with it. To that end, Tor bridges are alternative ways to enter the Tor network. Some are private. Many are public. Some are listed on the Tor homepage at https://bridges.torproject.org/. In a hostile environment, you can see the value in using it to your advantage as it makes it *much more* difficult for an ISP to know you're using Tor.

What Bridges Are Not

While not especially *unreliable*, they are certainly *less* reliable than regular Tor usage where performance goes. But the tradeoff may be in your best interest. Only you can decide if the performance hit is warranted. Here's how to do it in Whonix.

Bridges must be added manually since there is no auto-install method for Whonix, but it's not that difficult. You simply must enter them into the proper directory, like so:

/etc/tor/torrc.

If you're using a graphical Whonix-Gateway, then you need to browse to:

Start Menu -> Applications -> Settings -> /etc/tor/torrc.examples

To edit your torrc file (which is necessary for bridge adding), browse to:

Start Menu -> Applications -> Settings ->
/etc/tor/torrc

Then add whatever bridge you copied from the
Tor bridges page (or a private one if you have it).
Then restart Tor for it to take effect. If you run into
trouble (and most likely will if it's your first time) there
are a few forums to help you out. Forums that I've
found invaluable are the following:

Whonix Forum
https://www.whonix.org/forum/

Tor Reddit
http://www.reddit.com/r/TOR/

Wilders Security Forum
http://www.wilderssecurity.com/search/2697759/?
q=whonix&o=date

Quora
http://www.quora.com/Tor

Tor and VPNs

It seems that there's a lot of confusion among beginners when it comes to VPN companies. Are they anonymous? Which ones? Are any operated by the government? People read one thing and see something else in the media that contradicts that one thing, so who's right?

The cold, hard truth about VPN companies, is that a few want your patronage so badly that bury the fine print on their web page where it's difficult to read. Believe me, that's fine print that you need to see. It really is a minefield where some of these companies are concerned.

For this reason, you need to decide whether you want privacy or anonymity. They're different beasts that require different setups. Privacy is easier. Anonymity, not so much. One is like wearing Frodo's ring. The other is crafting it. The most confusing part is that not every VPN user uses Tor, and not every Tor user uses a VPN service. Regardless, it's advantageous to combine two powerful tools; one that affords privacy (the VPN) and one anonymity (Tor).

For what it's worth, if you like this combo then you must find a VPN that offers 128-bit encryption and that doesn't store **activity logs**. That's the first rule of business.

And the part where the fine print comes in. Many VPN companies *claim* they don't log a thing... but will gladly offer your subscriber data on a silver platter if a subpoena demands it. Between Big Money and Your Freedom, big money always wins. They will never go to jail for you. Ever. So do your due diligence and research beyond what you see in forums, since many of these companies outsource fake reviewers to write up glowing comments about them.

Now then. Obviously a VPN service is not anonymous by default. Providers love to tout that it is, but let's face it, there's nothing anonymous about using someone else's line if you left a money trail leading straight to your front door.

Enter Tor, slayer of gremlins and we-know-what-is-better-for-you nanny staters. Tor makes for an extra and formidable layer of security in that the thieves must go an extra step to steal from you. Thieves come in all flavors, from simple jewel thieves to border guards who want to make you as miserable as they are. So it's a good idea to ensure all the holes in your Tor installation are filled and the system is updated correctly.

Updated applications are resistant to malware attacks since it takes time to find exploitable holes in the code. Only if you don't update, then it doesn't matter which VPN you use with Tor since your session can be **compromised**. Here is what you can do:

Option 1

<u>Pay for a VPN anonymously</u>

This means no credit cards. No verified phone calls. No links to you or anyone you know. In fact, leave no money trail to your real name or city or livelihood at all... and never connect to the VPN without Tor.

For optimal anonymity, connect to your VPN through Tor using Tails. Even if the VPN logs every session, if you *always* use Tor with Tails, it would take an extremely well-funded adversary to crack that security chain. Without logging, it's even more secure.

But always <u>assume they log</u>.

Option 2

<u>Pay for a VPN using a credit card</u>

Connecting with Tor when using a card with your name on it does nothing for anonymity. It's fine for privacy, but not for anonymity. This is good if you want to use Pandora in Canada for instance, but not if you want to hire a contract killer to loosen Uncle Frick's lips a bit. Uncle Frick, who is 115 years of age and being tight-lipped on where the sunken treasure is.

VPN services sometimes get a bad rap by anonymity enthusiasts, but signing up *anonymously* for a VPN has advantages. It strengthens the anonymity when using Tor, for one.

Even if the VPN keeps logs of every user, they'll not know even with a court order the real identity of the user in question. Yet if you used Paypal, Bitcoin, credit cards or any other identifiable payment method to subscribe to a VPN for the express purpose of using Tor, then anonymity is weakened since these leave a paper trail. And just so you know, using Bitcoin by itself is not 100% anonymous. Nothing really is. But you can get very close; say, 98%, if you implement good OPSEC along with good security practices.

The real down and dirty gutter downside is .onion sites. These are sites that can only be accessed by using Tor. The problem is that the last link of connectivity for these sites needs to be Tor, not the VPN. You'll understand what is involved once you connect with one. This brings us to our next question:

How Tor Friendly is the VPN?

That depends on you. Spammers use Tor. Hackers use Tor. Identity thieves use Tor. A few VPNs have reservations about letting users attain that elusive 98% anonymity by signing up anonymously. But if you did sign up anonymously, then you've little to fear since at that point it is *their* butts on the line.

Only there's one problem: the hardliners at the FBI don't like this. In fact they'd just as soon go after you if you use a VPN over Tor. Might a person come under twice the suspicion by using both? Maybe.

From Fee.org

"The investigative arm of the Department of Justice is attempting to short-circuit the legal checks of the Fourth Amendment by requesting a change in the Federal Rules of Criminal Procedure. These procedural rules dictate how law enforcement agencies must conduct criminal prosecutions, from investigation to trial. Any deviations from the rules can have serious consequences, including dismissal of a case. The specific rule the FBI is targeting outlines the terms for obtaining a search warrant.

It's called Federal Rule 41(b), and the requested change would allow law enforcement to obtain a warrant to search electronic data without providing any specific details as long as the target computer location has been hidden through a technical tool like Tor or a virtual private network. It would also allow nonspecific search warrants where computers have been intentionally damaged (such as through botnets, but also through common malware and viruses) and are in five or more separate federal judicial districts. Furthermore, the provision would allow investigators to seize electronically stored information regardless of whether that information is stored inside or outside the court's jurisdiction.

The change may sound like a technical tweak, but it is a big leap from current procedure."

The NSA does this without hindrance. We know from Snowden's leaks that the FBI uses the NSA's metadata from private citizen's phone records. Thus, a VPN is not a truly formidable obstacle to them.

But this takes it to an entirely different level since if merely *signing up* for a VPN provides a basis for a legal search, then they can snoop on any ISP's server they want with no legal grounds at all to justify it. They've done similar things in Brazil.

But here in the good ole U.S.A, it usually goes down like this:

1.) Spy on JoBlo to see what he's up to.

2.) Make justification to seize his PC or raid him by reconstructing the case to fit the agenda.

3.) Apply pressure to the right people with direct access to subscriber info.

4.) Subpoena to decrypt subscriber's data. If they've done it once, they can do it a hundred more times. No big deal.

Solution:

If you're going to go the VPN route, then use PGP, also known as Pretty Good Privacy. Never, ever transmit plain data over a VPN, not even one that offers SSL.

Final thoughts:

1.) Talking to police will never help you, not even in a raid situation where you're hoodwinked. They (Homeland, possibly) wake you at gunpoint at 6AM and corral your family into the living room and threaten to take everyone to jail unless someone confesses. It's all lies, all the time.

A friend once remarked that a plain-clothes officer once knocked on his door to ask him if he was using Tor, only to *make sure he wasn't doing anything illegal*. He answered, "Yes, but nothing illegal, sir."

That gave incentive to go forward like a giant lawnmower right over his hairline. He was proven innocent later on, but not before the cops dragged his reputation through the mud. No public apology came. They rarely do.

2.) If they don't charge you for running a hidden service, walk out. In fact, if they don't charge you with *anything*... walk out. Every word out of your mouth will aid them, not you.

3.) You have no reason to justify anything done in your own home to them, or anyone else. The responsibility of proving guilt rests on their shoulders, not yours.

If you're in a situation where you have to talk or give up your encrypted laptop, always *always* give up your laptop first. Laptops are cheap and easy to replace. Five years is not.

Using Bitcoins to Signup Anonymously to a VPN Service

Bitcoins are not designed for absolute anonymity, but neither are VPNs. They're designed for privacy. So why use them?

Well because any extra layer that strengthens your anonymity is a layer you want. But just as with any advanced tool, you can lessen anonymity if you get careless with it. Good, tight anonymity tools can be a bane or a boon: A boon provided you do your homework. If not, folly and embarrassment ensues, maybe even a situation where, depending on the country you're in, you might as well slap the cuffs on yourself. It's sad that the times have come to this predicament.

So let's consider then how one pays for a VPN and obtains this level of absolute anonymity - recognizing that a VPN **by itself** will do nothing to further this goal. It is only one tool in a toolbox full of expertise and Bitcoin is only one of them as well. You wouldn't try to repair a Camaro engine with only a wrench, would you?

Onto Bitcoin...

Bitcoins are open source coins, a digital currency that utilizes P2P-like code and, like *real* money, you can buy online products with it. Products like memory cards at Newegg or even a Usenet or VPN premium service. These are useful to us. Using these Bitcoins, you the end-user, completely bypass the need for a credit union or a bank. That's the good news, but they've got some disadvantages. More on that in a moment.

For now, simply know that they're created from the collective CPU computations of a matrix of users (like you) who donate to their creation. Bitcoin mining is involved and though you may have seen images of Bitcoins on websites stamped with a golden "B", they're actually not something you can carry around in your pocket yet. Not in the way you think, at least.

They've something in common with PGP - public and private keys - just like the PGP application, only instead of verifying your identity like PGP does, Bitcoins verify your *balance*. This is where **Bitcoin wallets** come in. Again, this isn't a magic bullet, but rather one specialized tool at our disposal beyond a mere wrench.

On that point, Bitcoin Wallets will only get better at strengthening anonymity in the coming years. They'll accomplish this by breaking the trail to our real identities since their development is constantly evolving to counteract attacks.

However as we mentioned earlier-- embarrassment will result if you neglect to do your homework; for every purchase by a particular wallet **can be traced**. That's right. If you buy a new video card at Newegg with it, the same that holds your credit card details, and then subscribe to a Usenet service or VPN, guess what: you've now established a trail to your real identity. The FBI or Chinese or Secret Shadow Government with Cigarette Man leading the charge will have no need of baying bloodhounds to sniff you out.

But not if you make only one purchase per wallet.

This means never using it for *any* online entity in which you've purchased goods while your real IP is connected. It also means forgoing Google Plus, Facebook, Skype and all social media outlets with said wallet. Twitter, Wal-Mart, BestBuy and even small mom & pop stores with multi-social media buttons splattered all over their websites - these are enemies of anonymity whether they know it or not (more likely they don't). They're not our friends any more than a grenade is your friend after pulling the pin.

A single individual may hold several addresses and make only two purchases a year, but if he cross-contaminates it by mixing up (each transaction is recorded in the Bitcoin blockchain), then anonymity is weakened and in most cases, destroyed by his own making. That's not good.

The trick is this: <u>don't create a pattern</u>. A string of purchases create a pattern; the exact sort of pattern Google and Amazon code into their algorithms to search and better target you with interest-based ads. That's bad for anonymity and that's far from the worse that can happen.

We get around this problem by using **Bitcoin mixers**. These weaken the links between several different Bitcoin addresses, since the history of that purchase is wiped by the exchange of Bitcoins among other Bitcoin users.

Bitcoin Wallets

In order to subscribe to a VPN or buy anything online with Bitcoins, a Bitcoin wallet is required. The good news is that more than one type is available to us. We'll go through each and list their pros and cons to better help you decide which is for you.

Desktop Wallet

A Desktop Wallet is what I use and for good reason: I have absolute control over it not to mention the thought of having to access my money on someone else's web server defeats the entire notion of anonymity. I would never store my encrypted files "in the cloud," and neither should you. At least, not without an insanely secure system.

Think about it. Would you bury your safe in the neighbor's yard with a For Sale sign out front? It's the same deal here with a number of not-too-comforting scenarios that could materialize: The server could go down. The company could go bankrupt. Any person on the other end on the hosting side could, theoretically at least, install a keylogger without your knowledge. And believe me those nasty buggers are a pain in the patella to get rid of once you've got it.

Desktop wallets aren't perfect, mind you, but they're way better than trusting anything to The Cloud. One downside, however, is that you must backup your Bitcoin wallet; an especially imperative task as it may contain a lot of money. I do this quite religiously every week, as should you, and not just with Bitcoin-related data but *all* my data. The motto I like to follow is, 'If it's not backed up to three different forms of media, then it's not backed up." Works for me.

My apologies if this all sounds like a Sunday sermon, but some of this stuff really must be taken as gospel truth, and I only wished someone would've told me years ago never to trust just one backup.

Mobility/Travel Wallet

Next we come to the Travel Wallet. As the name implies, you carry this on you to make purchases in the same way you would a credit card. It makes for great convenience if you travel internationally.

There are many types of wallets that fall into this category, such as <u>Coinbase</u> and <u>Electrum</u>, but I found <u>Multibit</u> to be the easiest to learn. It's available in both Linux and Windows flavors and offers a pass phrase option. Even the balance sheet looks like a PGP interface. Yet it's very beginner friendly and open-source, so no worries about installed backdoors. It's also rock-solid for the purposes of anonymity.

You can check it out for yourself here:

<u>https://www.multibit.org/en/help/v0.5/help_getting</u> <u>Started.html</u>

Multibit Windows Install

Now we come to the instructions for a clean install of this work of wonder. First off,

- Download the Windows installer from multibit.org.

- Run the installer.

A possible problem we may run into is that, on Windows 7 64-bit - which is the system of choice outside of Linux these days - it may be that the Java Virtual Machine (JVM) is not correctly located, or "Failed to create a selector" is shown in the error message. If this happens, you need to change the compatibility setting via the shortcut:

- Choose the compatibility dialog (right click--> icon - Properties --> Compatibility)
- Choose: "Run this program in compatibility mode for Windows XP SP3."

- Check the box: "Run this program as an administrator"

Multibit Linux Install

This can be a little daunting if you've never used Linux before. So now's a good time to learn since Linux gives you far more control than Windows. If you're a Linux fan to begin with (and you should be if anonymity is something you want), then download the Linux / Unix installer at the Multibit.org website.

- Next, open a terminal window and create an installer executable with:

chmod +x multibit-0.5.18-linux.jar

- Now run the installer: java -jar multibit-0.5.18-linux.jar

- Then Install.

Afterwards, you'll have a shortcut to start MultiBit in your "Applications | Other" menu. If you see no MultiBit shortcut, you can run MultiBit manually by doing the following:

- Open a terminal window and 'cd' to your installation directory and type java -jar multibit-exe.jar

Now then. We come to the point where it is time to purchase some Bitcoins. There are a few useful guides around which list possible advantages unique to your geography.

As you can see from the link, there are several options, but what we want to do is execute an offline option; to buy Bitcoins *off the grid* - which cannot be traced. Cash only, so to speak.

The LocalBitcoins site looks promising, as does TradeBitcoin. But as Trade looks offline, let's go with LocalBitcoins.

- After you choose a Bitcoin outfit, you must signup for the site (anonymously) but be aware of the interest charges which vary from one to another depending on how much you want to deal in. For this transaction, use an email in which you anonymously signed up. That means:

- Using Tor Browser and/or Tails setup
- No Facebook or other Social Media Search cookies present on your machine
- And finally, use one that's only been accessed for Tor or Bitcoins.

Choose 'Purchase' on the seller's page and the amount you wish to buy. Remember, we're not buying a house here, only a VPN to use with Tor. Once funds are transferred out of escrow, you'll be notified.

Notice that the trader you are dealing with might be able to see your financial information, i.e. which bank you use, but you can always opt to meet up in person if you want. This carries a whole other set of offline risks which are far too deep a topic for this book (though my Invisibility Toolkit book goes into this on an international level).

Lastly, verify that the funds are in your Bitcoin Wallet before going any further.

Paying for the VPN to Use with Tor

Now it's time to pay for your VPN service... *anonymously*. Let's choose Air VPN at $9 dollars per month, and who also accepts Bitcoins for payment.

First: Sign up for the service, but do not put any information that you've used on any other site. Info such as usernames or passwords. Also, since we don't need to input any banking info, no money trail will be traced to us. The email we use is a throwaway email, one that you, hopefully at least, used Tor to sign up with.

Second: Give them the wallet address for our Bitcoin payment. Hit send.

Your Done!

Like any Usenet service, a VPN service will send confirmation to your email with details you need to use that service. Afterward you can see the details of this payment in your Bitcoin wallet.

As you can see, a Ph.D in Computer Science is not needed for this extra layer of anonymity. The problem with the mass of people on Tor, however, is that they cannot be bothered to do these simple extra steps. That's bad for them. Good for you. Those that wear extra armor are often the ones left standing after a long battle. It's true that warriors with heavier armor can't swing a sword as fast as though with light armor, and they can't run as fast, but then they don't really need to. That's the whole point.

At any rate, there's but one little topic left to discuss, and it's the most important:

Using Your Real Name Online Outside of Tor

This is a big one, one that I'm guilty of breaking. I've since forgiven myself because now I know that even anonymity nuts can crack under peer pressure. Every now and then we do something galactically dumb - like use Facebook over Tor (thanks Grandma). Regardless, one question that she asked at the time - which kept hounding me like a baying dog back then - was this:

What kind of danger is there in using your real name online?

I hate to say it but even with all I've learned the answer is still the same now as it was way back when Facebook first hit the scene. In fact, I suspect it's the same now as it was in my early teens when I crept around an online watering hole called The Well.

The answer is: It depends.

Law enforcement and prospective employers who'll mine your social media profiles for data are often worse than the thieves who rob you in broad daylight. They salivate when you announce on Twitter you'll be out of town for two weeks. Then they strike and strike fast. Thieves, while unsavory brutes who're often dullards to be sure, are more honest in their profession than a lot of the corporate behemoths that do things behind your back.

Employers are the worst of the lot. As hypocritical as Harvey Two-Face. They demand transparency in *your* life but *never their own*. Make an inflamed political post or drink wine on vacation in Bora Bora with half-naked Filipinas and those fire-twirlers doing their thing and you could lose your job... or even be *denied* one. Not kidding. It happens to people you'd least expect in places that seemed like the Eden. Likewise, if you mention on your resume that you use Tor, that's a red flag. It's not only Google that gives Tor the stink eye. You may even one day hear this from an employer in an interview:

"I noticed you're a big fan of Tor and other anonymity tools that shield your IP address and

prevent better relationships between consumers and companies... Could you elaborate on why you need to use an anonymizing service? We like transparency in our employees and in our consumers."

Truthfully, your answer can sound like something Einstein said on his best hair day and it can still rub them the wrong way, especially if you take pride in it or worse, rub their noses in it as I did.

Yes, I was actually tasked with explaining why I liked Tor in an interview. And all for a position that handled a lot of money. Putting aside for a moment the fact that Tor is not suitable for counterfeiting or bank theft, as soon as she said 'consumer', I knew what she really thought of me. That, my friend, was the dead giveaway.

Consumer is a word meant for the animal kingdom like male or female. Squirrels, for instance, or masked raccoons or other garbage thieving vermin. You know, beasts that roam on all fours and are slaves to instinct. Beasts that don't pray, forgive or sing praises to a Higher Being they can neither feel, see, nor hear. That's what I thought of when she used that word.

I'm thankful for the upfront honesty, actually, but what really bothered me was the casual way it was asked, like every applicant should have something to hide if they like anonymous communications. Like some wet-behind-the-ears greased up code monkey in the hacker clan Anonymous and up to no good. At any rate, she didn't like my answer.

"Because I value freedom."

That sunk my battleship. I came out of that interview perplexed, yet jobless, viewing privacy as somewhat of a double-edged sword since one *needs* an online presence for many higher paying employers. It didn't sit well with me in the long run. I felt a little cheated to be honest, and as I drove home some of the mumblings I'd overheard later on became as loud as roaring trains in my ears. Here's a few tidbits:

- Don't like someone on Facebook? You probably won't like working with them.

- Like the competitor's products? Here's our three-year non-compete agreement for you to sign.

- You use Tor? The only people that use that are terrorists, pedos and hitmen. You must be one of those buggers.

Soon thereafter, any time a prospective employer noticed "Tor" under the Hobbies section of my resume, it would always illicit a negative response. Like witchcraft or Dungeons and Dragons Dungeonmaster. My breathing seemed to become erratic as my heart raced, as if they were about to summon an unbadged "authority" to warn me of being *too private*.

He'd be dressed like Dilbert, only skinnier and with a bumblebee-yellow pen and a clipboard. He'd have multiple facial tics and that annoying eyebrow raise, as if it were completely illogical to value privacy. I have no idea why he'd have a clipboard, but he always did in my minds eye.

My solution was to divide my public and private identity in social settings and remove any trace of it on my resume. In fact, I refused to give any indication on any social media site, either, that I was into any of the following:

- PGP
- Encryption, or encrypting files or Operating Systems
- Tor Relays
- I2P
- Freenet
- Anonymity in general
- *Anything* linked to Edward Snowden

Such is the nature of the masses. One simply cannot rely on Facebook or Twitter or Google to respect one's freedom to use Tor without announcing it to the whole world. But at least with Tor, Google cannot mine your browsing session for ads. No ads = no soup for them. From NBC:

"The Internet search giant is changing its terms of service starting Nov. 11. Your reviews of restaurants, shops and products, as well as songs and other content bought on the Google Play store could show up in ads that are displayed to your friends, connections and the broader public when they search on Google. The company calls that feature "shared endorsements."

So I firewall everything I do. I use Ghostery for social sites and offer only pseudonymous details about myself. In fact, I try to avoid any correlation between Tor and any social media site just as one would a can of gasoline and a lighted match.

Anonymous Bullies

Let's talk about anonymity and bullies for a moment, and how identification does nothing to alleviate any kind of bullying.

The media, along with Google and Facebook, seem to think that if only everyone's name were known to them, then every bully from California to Florida would go up in smoke quicker than those three hoodlum bullies from The Neverending Story. Sadly, I suspect it'd never be that easy.

Bullies are a lot like vampires. They either take a lot of life all at once, or drain you dry one nibble at a time (if you're the romantic Twilight strain). And if you've ever read anything by Anne Rice, then you know that every clan is as different as diamonds are to lumps of coal. One thing they do share are similar *beginnings*. Adolescence, for example. Were you ever bullied in school?

I was.

I remember every spiked-club wielding ogre who pelted me into nothing but a wet snowball in 7th grade. Only it didn't stop there. How I wished it had, but I knew Aladdin's lamp was half a world away, hidden in some tomb I could never hope to break into. So I watched as bullies spread like a plague, every one of them sludging upward to other grades like a blob working it's way up the school staircase in search of easier victims. Ninth on upward to 12th and even into the workforce, it seemed, was the modus operandi. Bullies who'd make great orc chieftains if there were any openings, such was their cruelty.

I recall one particularly nasty breed of ogre in 8th grade. A mutant who was the worst of the lot. A walking colossus who sweat when he ate as though he being assimilated by The Thing. His head was so big, I thought for sure if it were ever separated from the rest of his body that it would crawl away like a sea crab only to mutate somewhere else. Another school, possibly. When he arced an arm over me at the water fountain, it sounded like a double-bladed axe prepping to slice the air in half.

Harassment grew more fierce every year. Later, I'd learn that his entire family, perhaps his entire *generation*, grew up being the baddest of the bad - bullies that thrived on terrorizing to make a name for themselves. Every one of them went on to become cops in the New Orleans area. One died of diabetes. Another went on to join the ATF to fight the evil scourge called *drugs*.

Where does anonymity come into this? Well for starters, I knew everything about these cretins, and I don't mean just their names. I knew who their parents were. What they did for a living. Who they hung out with. What beers their dad's drank and what porn they stored in their garages. Gossip spread like wildfire in high school and no detail of identifying information was ever left out, certainly not in the boy's locker room where rare Penthouse editions could make or break a boy's reputation.

Tell the school admins, you're thinking. That's exactly what I did, and did so with an intense 'snitchy' feeling as I forked over all the data I had on them. All the gory details. All the evidence. Every 'Thing' victim who'd no doubt one day turn into Big Things like the bullies were. I even gave data to the Superintendent, a great big firestorm lady named Beverly, with red curls that slithered around her head like Medusa's snakes. Her former job, I learned, was working in some HR high-rise pushing others around. I remember multiple times meeting her in that office and walking away seeing gold sparkling everywhere due to all the trophies. It gave me migraines.

Meetings between my circus acrobat of a mother became fruitless and rather embarrassing, especially when I threatened to make myself 'disappear'. They (incorrectly) thought that meant I was planning on stringing myself up from the nearest tree. I just sulked and took it like a 13 year old champ. I'd later learn from martial arts that sometimes, when the crowd is looking, you just have to take a beating and wait for a later opportunity.

At any rate, absolutely nothing positive came of it despite all the identifying data. Yep... nothing came of it even as I knew **everything** about the scourge I and many others faced daily. Knowing the parents of the darling orclings did nothing. Knowing their names did nothing. Knowing how many other kids they tormented did nothing and, let's face it, kids just aren't smart enough to band together and build flamethrowers no matter how many times they've watched The Road Warrior.

We can see how bullying spreads on Facebook. It spreads like anthrax. Little wolves ostracize a rejected member when a drop of fear is shown, so they crucify without knowing much of anything about him or why he's being targeted. Real names? Check. Real addresses? Yep. Everything is traceable now just as it was way back then. Only now it is far easier since so few kids know how to hide their online footprints.

And still the orcs came with angry faces eager to make an example of the one who snitched. Like sharks to a wounded dolphin.

When I hear of 15 year olds in the UK hanging themselves in mom's bedroom to escape the torture, one thing is immediately obvious: what they really want is to *disappear*. Just like I did. They want *anonymity*.

But that's not something bullies think highly of. Quite simply, they won't allow it. Neither do they allow running away. Not really. Not that a kid has the means anyway when you factor in finance: No money. No car. No distant relatives in Alaska to run away with and hunt moose all winter.

Anonymity, therefore, shouldn't be outlawed. It shouldn't even be an option. It should be a personal right. It should be the law on some level, except that it isn't. This is because if they ever gave us true anonymity, they, in whatever form current bullies take, would lose the precious power they wield. The greatest irony is that bullying itself makes the bully slave to the bullying. It makes him a slave to pain.

If Google and Facebook ever teamed up with the federal government to require ID to access the internet, we'd all be better off going face-to-face with an Alaskan grizzly.

Email Anonymity

At the risk of sounding like some grumpy old red dragon who lives up in the mountains... I miss the old days.

There was a time when one needn't worry about things said in hushed emails. Security? That was something a few geeks argued about on Usenet or backroom bulletin boards. Altavista and Infoseek were the search engines and targeted ads were something you did on your own with banner sites. Email was safe back then as were the ads. You clicked or didn't click. No snooping necessary to make money. Sadly, no longer.

Advertising and search engines now tailor advertisements to individuals based on what you like and are sure to click, and they count on you not caring. So they don't push too hard. They just slip in a little snake venom here and there whenever you click through a new Privacy Policy for the new Google or Kindle app. Soon, you become immune to all the poison that's been injected into your veins as they build up a tolerance, and all under the radar.

When a trailer is leaked or someone says something nasty about the government, you can bet IP addresses have been subpoenaed before you finish reading the article. Sometimes I imagine a lot of ex-Soviet officers are laughing at how many snitches the Internet produces on a yearly basis. Subversion to the extreme. In light of this, I began to research if it was at all possible to send a message that is *foolproof* against subpoenas? Something untraceable?

As it turns out, there's more than one way to skin a cat, and there are many flavors to choose from to accomplish this task. Below are a few rock-solid services that, when combined with Tor, build a veritable shield around you online. A virtual fortress.

Anonymity squared if your message is encrypted and you don't trade in state secrets or plan to assassinate world leaders.

The first is **TorGuard**.

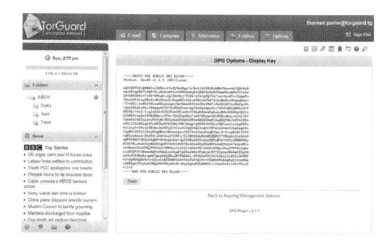

TorGuard allows users to use PGP (Pretty Good Privacy) in email so you needn't worry about snooping. You get 10MB plus several layers of protection with mobility support.

Second is W3, The Anonymous Remailer

Connectable with Tor, you only need an email address to send the message to (preferably encrypted with PGP--more on that in a moment).

Another is Guerrilla Mail. They allow users to create throwaway emails to be used at leisure. Emails sent are immediately wiped from the system after you hit Send. Well, within one hour at any rate.

All of these services claims of anonymity would be pretty thin if we failed to encrypt our messages - which brings us to PGP.

PGP is the encryption standard of choice for many old users like myself, and for good reason. It's never been cracked by the NSA or FBI or any intelligence agency, and likely won't until quantum computers become so commonplace that you see them installed at stoplights. It works by way of key pairs, one public and one private (the one you will use to decrypt your messages with).

You needn't worry though when you hear the term "keys". It's not difficult to grasp and it'll be as easy as hitting send once you've done it a few times.

The first thing you must do is make your public key <u>available</u>. This is only used to verify your identity and is not the same as divulging your passphrase for say, a Drivecrypt container. Your recipient must also share with you their key so you can respond in turn.

That sounds technical and it is, but there's quite a silver lining: Only the two of you will be able to read each other's messages. The dark side is if the other person is compromised and you don't know about it. If that's the case, neither will he if he's got a keylogger, in which the powers that be can read everything you encrypt. But let's stick with the basics before we jump into a discussion on how to decrypt the Matrix as we know it.

1.) To begin, make two keys, one public - for everyone else but you -and one that you wouldn't dream of sharing with your own mother. You should back this key up in a secure medium, and remember that if it isn't backed up to three different types of media, it isn't backed up (sorry if I sound like a broken record here). If your truly paranoid, send one on an encrypted microSD to your parents in case of house fire. Yes, it does happen and will happen when you least expect it.

2.) If you opt to tell mom, then she'll need your public key (you did publish it on a public key server, right? Get it here: http://pgp.mit.edu/)

After which, you can read it by way of your private key. She doesn't know this key so you can relax about her posting it on the fridge.

3.) You can "sign" any message you want over Tor or anywhere else (Freenet, for example, the highest security setting of which demands absolute trust of your friend's darknet connection) to verify it is really you sending it.

Unless Norman Bates does a shower scene on you and takes your key physically, you're pretty secure. Your mom can then verify with your public key that it's really you.

4.) Users you've messaged with (or not) can sign your public key as a way of verifying your identity. As you've probably guessed, the more people that do this, that is, *vouch for you*, the better.

Important:

Unless you've got the photographic memory of Dustin Hoffman in Rainman, it's a good idea to store your public/private keys and passwords and also revocation-certificate to backup media, so you can retrieve it five years down the line should you need it. And believe me, you will!

Encrypt them in containers. Always print your key-file or pass phrase and deposit in a safe place. If you lose it, all documents encrypted with it are permanently lost. There are no back-doors and no way to decrypt without it. Also consider making an expiration date at key-pair creation.

If you like nice and easy interfaces, try Mymail-Crypt for Google's Gmail. It is a plugin that allows users to use PGP-encrypted messages in a handy interface, though ensure your browser is air-tight secure and you trust it with your private key.

One other thing

Rather than having to encrypt files and upload them somewhere unsafe, look at an app called AxCrypt. It's an encryption tool that's useful if you're used to uploading to Dropbox or Google Drive. Just remember that in the event you upload an encrypted file to "The Cloud," you will not know if your password to said file has been compromised without setting strict security rules. With that said, let's configure PGP for Windows.

- First, install Gpg4Win at Gpg4win.org.

- Next, create your key in Kleopatra (kde.org) and choose Export-Certificate-to-Server by right click so you can publish it to a keyserver. Get a trusted friend to "sign" and establish trust. This is just the beginning of a long, secure friendship.

- Use Claws-Mail client that comes packaged with it, or use Enigmail if you're using Thunderbird.

- Send a few messages back and forth to your trusted friend via PGP to get the hang of things.

- Optionally you can set a Yahoo/Gmail/Hotmail filter so as to forward any messages that contain "Begin PGP message" to a more private account.

Tor Instant Messaging Bundle

It is no secret that the NSA has Skype, Yahoo Chat and other instant message services in their hands, but as long as the Tor development team knows about it, they can respond in kind. Enter Tor Instant Messaging Bundle.

True anonymity is the goal of this application. It's built by the very same who developed the Tor browser bundle and like that application, will route all communication through Tor relays... encrypted *backwards and forwards* and hidden from the NSA's prying eyes.

There's also Torchat which you can get at Github.com. Torchat offers encrypted chat and even file-sharing and since it's built upon Tor, you're assured absolute privacy on what you say and to whom you say it. Both Windows and Mac versions are available and no install is necessary. Just unzip anywhere and run (preferably from an encrypted hard drive or USB-Drive) the blue earth symbol titled 'Torchat'.

There's a few more useful anonymity apps that are great for communicating incognito. The next is ChatSecure.

ChatSecure is mainly used for encrypted messaging on mobility devices, but they offer PC, Linux and Mac versions as well. They've some interesting comments on their website, one of which piqued my curiosity:

The Guardian Project creates easy to use secure apps, open-source software libraries, and customized mobile devices that can be used around the world by any person looking to protect their communications and personal data from unjust intrusion, interception and monitoring.

Whether your are an average citizen looking to affirm your rights or an activist, journalist or humanitarian organization looking to safeguard your work in this age of perilous global communication, we can help address the threats you face.

<u>Telegram</u> - This app also focuses on messaging but with superior speed and is similar to SMS and allows for picture/video sending. There are also 'Secret Chats' that offer encrypted sessions. They claim no data is kept on their servers and you can even set the app to permanently delete all messages.

<u>CryptoCat</u> - Billed as an alternative to social media chat apps like those seen on Facebook, Twitter and the like, CryptoCat gives you encrypted communications using the AES encryption standard. All encrypted info is deleted after an hour of inactivity.

<u>Freenet</u> - This is the granddaddy of all anonymous systems the world over, both for file sharing or any kind of secret chats. Explaining everything it has to offer goes far beyond our Tor discussion as they are two different systems, but I include it here as an alternative if you find Tor lacking.

And it is not as simple as Tor, nor is it as fast unless you leave it running 24/7. It's not for everyone though, as there are all manner of criminals that use it. You'll notice this if you load up any groups, as it's hard to ignore and unlike Usenet, there's no one to file a complaint with. No one to report. No Usenet authority to ban their account. It is pretty much the Wild West without a sheriff or much of anyone to round up a posse. Anarchy doesn't quite do it justice. But.. there are ways of lessening the damage which we'll get to in a moment.

Just know that for *absolute anonymity* and freedom of speech, there's no better tool to use if you have the patience to learn its darknet offerings. The following is from the website:

Freenet is free software which lets you anonymously share files, browse and publish "freesites" (web sites accessible only through Freenet) and chat on forums, without fear of censorship. Freenet is decentralised to make it less vulnerable to attack, and if used in "darknet" mode, where users only connect to their friends, is very difficult to detect.

Communications by Freenet nodes are encrypted and are routed through other nodes to make it extremely difficult to determine who is requesting the information and what its content is.

Users contribute to the network by giving bandwidth and a portion of their hard drive (called the "data store") for storing files. Files are automatically kept or deleted depending on how popular they are, with the least popular being discarded to make way for newer or more popular content. Files are encrypted, so generally the user cannot easily discover what is in his datastore, and hopefully can't be held accountable for it. Chat forums, websites, and search functionality, are all built on top of this distributed data store.

An important recent development, which very few other networks have, is the "darknet": By only connecting to people they trust, users can greatly reduce their vulnerability, and yet still connect to a global network through their friends' friends' friends and so on. This enables people to use Freenet even in places where Freenet may be illegal, makes it very difficult for governments to block it, and does not rely on tunneling to the "free world".

It's not as simple as using a Usenet provider's newsgroup reader. No sir, Freenet requires **patience**. Using Frost or Fuqid (Front End apps for the main Freenet program), it might be half an hour before you can "subscribe" to groups or download in the way you can Usenet. Some groups, like the Freenet group and other technical groups, will be immediately available but with few messages. Time will solve this. So keep it running in the closet and forget about it for a day or so if you plan on subscribing to a lot of groups. It'll be worth the wait.

Frost & Fuqid

Freenet by itself can be quite cumbersome to navigate with only a browser to guide you. The first time I used it, I felt the same way I did during Hurricane Katrina. As the storm began to rip the roof right off my house, I patted the walls looking for a light switch, like a blind person. It was like wandering around in a fog. I just wanted something that'd spark a light bulb in my head to make it all easier to grasp. Luckily, we've a few choices that'll simplify things, and the best two are free. The first is an external app named Frost. The second is Fuqid; two great front ends that'll help you communicate incognito.

Frost has seen a lot of improvements over the years, but I recommend you try Fuqid first as it's the first external app for Freenet that acts as an insert & download manager for files. Fuqid stands for: Freenet Utility for Queued Inserts and Downloads. It runs on both Windows or Linux under Wine. You really can't go wrong with either, but you should try both to see which fits your style.

The Fuqid freesite is on Freenet itself at:

USK@LESBxzEDERhGWQHI1t1av7CvZY9SZKG bCnsD7txqXOl,nP0CHuKvlbVzcrnz79TEd22E56IbKj-KHB-W8HHi9dM,AQACAAE/Fuqid/-1/

You will need to type the above Freenet USK key into Freenet's front control panel where it says "Key" to get it. Like anything else, it can take several minutes to load if you're new to Freenet.

After you've installed it, right click on the left side with your list of boards and choose "Add new board". For the name, put in "**fuqid-announce**" without the quotes. You'll now find a new board called "fuqid-announce" in your list of boards.

Now then. Right click this board and choose "Configure selected board". This'll bring up a new window. On that window click "Secure board" to change it from a public board. Now in the section that says "Public key" paste in the key below:

SSK@qoY-E5SKRu66pmKH64xa~R~w3hXmS5ZNtqnpEGoCVww,HTVcdWChaaebfRAublHSxBSRaRFG91qCwsa3mGF3-QE,AQACAAE

Now you have the announce board for Fuqid added to your Frost boards. The latest release of Fuqid will be posted to this board along with the fuqid board on FMS.

Questions? Direct them to the Frost or FMS board called Fuqid at https://wiki.freenetproject.org/FUQID.

Passwords

Good, strong passwords are like having a couple of Rottweilers sleeping in your den. Most intruders will leave as soon as the chaos starts, and as any Rottie owner will tell you, that's a storm you don't want to engage bare-handed unless you've got a couple of juicy steaks loaded up with sleeping powder. Weak passwords, on the other hand, are like having a Golden Retriever for a guard dog. They make good hunting companions if you shoot waterfowl, and are nice and easy to trust around kids, but they take the 'niceness' too far. They may just let out a little woof at 3AM when said intruder comes to relieve you of your $3000 laptop. Then your super awesome nice dog will hide under the coffee table (the dog, not the intruder). So much for chaos theory.

You've heard for years that you should never use anything personal as your password. Personal meaning family names, favorite books, favorite movies and so on. So then, how do we solve the problem of having a good strong password that we can remember?

Remix your passwords with a symbol or two. If you think a hacker won't be able to guess the name of your girlfriend's locker combination, you'd be mistaken. It's no effort at all to guess, even if you mix it up a bit. Computers devoted to this practice can guess many in less than a nanosecond.

But how do you remember a password for a site used over Tor that has symbols?

Easy. Use a passphrase that's simple to recall for you and only you. First, write out the first letter of each word, taking note of case and position. Then insert a few symbols. For instance, you could try the following:

Last Sunday, the wife bought me a Rolex watch and it was too ugly.

Which, when changed is:

LS,twbmarwaiw2u

The above pass is hard for a hacker to guess, but easy for you to remember... assuming you are good at substitution.

Changing Your Passwords

Provided you've followed the above to the letter, you shouldn't have to rotate out your passwords every 90 days. I'm sure you've heard from both sides of the aisle their say on the subject, but I believe research has proven that keeping a strong password (unless you've got proof of a compromise) is a safe bet.

A research paper from ACM/CCS titled, *"The Security of Modern Password Expiration: An Algorithmic Framework and Empirical Analysis"* illuminates this point:

Yinqian Zhang, Fabian Monrose and Michael Reiter came to the conclusion that changing passwords every few months did not, repeat, did NOT increase security, saying

- at least 41% of passwords can be broken offline from previous passwords for the same accounts in a matter of seconds, and five online password guesses in expectation suffices to break 17% of accounts.

....our evidence suggests it may be appropriate to do away with password expiration altogether, perhaps as a concession while requiring users to invest the effort to select a significantly stronger password than they would otherwise (e.g., a much longer passphrase). ....

In the longer term, we believe our study supports the conclusion that simple password-based authentication should be abandoned outright.

Let's go over some options for passwords.

Storing Passwords in Tor Browser

You may have noticed that the "Remember Password" option in Tor Browser is not available. Or so it seems... if you look at the privacy setting and alter the history setting to "remember history" and "remember passwords for sites," it will no longer be greyed out.

Diceware

If you must store passwords, a good option for a unique random one is Diceware, where you can get an expiry date for any password months from the date of creation. You can copy any password to a text file, then encrypt it and mail it to yourself or place on a removable encrypted drive or USB stick.

Remember: Tor does nothing to improve the security of your *system* to everyday attacks. It only improves security online, and even then only when used optimally. Tor has no idea if your version of Windows is unpatched or infected with a zero-day malware payload that infected it with a keylogger. This burden falls upon you, dear reader.

One way in which a hacker could guess your complex password is if they linked your Tor usage with non-Tor usage and compromised your passwords from a non-Tor site. It sounds implausible and unlikely, but it isn't to a hacker who does this every day. This is why you should never use the same usernames/passwords for Tor that you do for non-Tor activity.

Preventing Non-Tor Activity From Being Linked with Tor Activity

It's risky to browse different websites simultaneously and preserve anonymity since Tor might end up sending requests for each site over the same circuit. It's possible that the exit node may see the **correlation**.

Far better to browse one site at a time, and thereafter choose "New Identity" from the Tor button. Any previous circuits are not used for the new session. Further, if you want to isolate two different apps (that is, allow actions executed by one app to be isolated from the actions of another), you can allow them to use the same SOCKS port... but change the username and password. More at this link:
https://www.torproject.org/docs/faq.html.en#Need ToUseAProxy

Another option is to set an "isolation flag" for the SOCKS port. The Tor manual has suggestions for this but it will lead to lower performance over Tor. Personally I like to use Whonix. Two instances, two VMs. One of them runs Tor and the other with Tor Firefox.

Keyloggers

You might wonder what a keylogger has to do with Tor, or for that matter what a keylogger even is. You're not alone. In fact you'd be surprised how many people have never heard of them, and shocked how many technically-minded users consider them a non-issue.

In 2010 I caught up with an old childhood friend of mine I'd not seen in over a decade. I learned he was now an ATF agent. It came as a surprise, as I'd (falsely) assumed his extensive training meant he knew as much as a systems analyst when it came to computer security. I was wrong. He replied to a post I made on a technical forum regarding the hacking group "Anonymous."

"What's a keylogger?" he asked. I waited for someone else to reply. No one did, so it fell to me. He seemed amazed, dumbfounded even, as though it were something only recently unleashed upon the net. I then told him that they'd been around a long time and that anti-virus programs have difficulty in removing them. Not only that, but that Windows was almost always on the receiving end of them.

Still, he's not alone as there's a lot of confusion on what they do exactly. Some call them spyware. Others call them trojans. Still others, exploits. They're a little bit of everything bad to be honest, with the kicker being that the FBI likes to use them when investigating organized crime. I've nothing against that, except when a custom payload coded by a federally employed programmer leaks said payload. Then you've got problems.

Keyloggers are *surveillance* software that tracks and records every click you make, every website visited, every keystroke typed. Chats, Skype, Emails. If you can type it, it can record it and all right under your very nose. It can even email what you type to a recipient on the other side of the world. CC numbers, passwords and Paypal login details are just the short list of targets it can acquire. You can see how valuable such a tool would be in bringing down a network of cartel members.

So how does one get in infected? By doing any of the following:

- Opening an email attachment
- Running an .exe file from a P2P network from an untrusted user
- Accessing an infected website with an outdated browser
- Intelligence agencies

Some employers use them to track productivity of employees. Some wives attach a hardware keylogger which can be bought online, via USB...to catch their spouse in the act. Parents use them on the kid's computer. As you can see, it isn't like they're 100% malicious *all the time*.

But they are difficult to detect. They wield an almost vampiric presence, but like vampires, there are subtle signs you can glean without whipping out a wooden stake (i.e. reformatting the hard drive).

Vampire Signs

- Sluggish browsing speed
- Laggy mouse/pausing keystrokes in a text doc
- Letters don't match on display with what you type
- Errors on multiple webpages when loading heavy text/graphics

There are two types of Keyloggers, and they're both capable of catastrophic damage if you use Tor. The first is the software variant.

Software Keyloggers

This type hides inside your operating system and thrive in Windows. Linux, not so much because of the sheer control Linux gives you. Hence the better security.

The keylogger records keystrokes and sends them to a hacker or other criminal at set times, provided the computer is online. Cloaked, most users will never see it working its dark art. Many popular anti-virus vendors have trouble identifying it because the mechanisms of deployment change so frequently.

Hardware Keyloggers

Every spy film has used one of these. Bond. Bourne. Even Ethan in Mission Impossible. Being hardware, it's a physical extension that can plug into any USB on a PC and can be bought online by suspecting spouses or kids wanting access to their dad's PC. Keystrokes are logged to ram memory, so no install is needed.

Unless you're the type to check behind your PC every day with a flashlight, you might not spot it until it's too late. They also can be built right into the keyboard. The FBI loves swapping the target's keyboard out with a custom-built surveillance device. Granted, this is mainly for high-value targets like the Mafia, but they're available to anyone.

Keylogger Prevention

- Check your keyboard for suspicious attachments. If you are an employee at X company and a new keyboard arrives at your desk one morning, exercise caution unless you trust your boss 200%.

- Use a Virtual Keyboard. No keystrokes = no logging!

- Use Guarded ID (http://www.guardedid.com/) to prevent hackers from capturing your keystrokes. It works by scrambling everything you type. This renders any info useless to hackers.

- Use a decent firewall to stop a keylogger from delivering your data. A year ago, my Comodo firewall alerted me to suspicious network activity seemingly out of nowhere when I wasn't doing anything online. Turns out I had the Win64/Alureon trojan.

Other Anti-Keyloggers

The following are not all free, but they should be.

Zemana AntiLogger (Free)

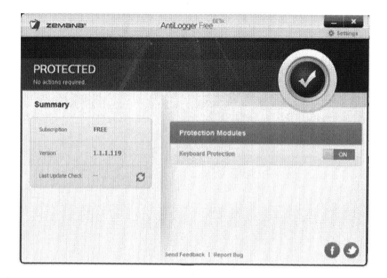

This "free" version is a bare-bones keylogger-detector. In fact it's quite stripped down. But if all you require is being alerted then this might be for you. The Keylog Guard offers encryption for all things typed at the keyboard. Any snooper will only get garbled letters from you.

SpyShelter STOP-LOGGER

The Free version offers more than Zemana does in that you get screenshot capture. It will also alert you to any code that tries to swipe your keystrokes from you but the Free version is not 64-bit compatible. It is $24.99.

Be aware, however, that removing a keylogger is nasty business. They have a habit of reinstalling themselves and will often hide as a service in svchost.exe. Task manager isn't much help without a dedicated app to save your system. The optimal way of prevention is to stop them in their tracks before insertion.

Darknet Markets

Some of you might be wondering how safe a so-called 'darknet' really is in light of the Tor vulnerabilities discussed. The short answer is: *As safe as you make it.*

When push comes to shove, you are the weakest link. Your own worst enemy. The last link in the security chain cannot be broken without your having played some part in the breaking of it. Pride goeth before a fall, so to speak. U.S. prisons are packed to the gills with those who let success go to their heads. Bank robbers, for instance, can be the biggest blunderers since the Apple Dumpling gang. They blow it all the time. It's how they get caught. An FBI agent once told me that even with a bank's state-of-the-art surveillance systems, thieves with any ounce of intelligence will almost always get away with it the first time.

Why?

Because fear motivates them to do it right the first time. To not make fatal mistakes. This fear slowly dissolves as they get more successful on each hit. It's the same thing with darknets, where overconfidence can kill you quicker than strychnine.

Overconfidence. It's like swigging moonshine when you think about it. A little bit can alienate others because they'll see your inflated ego in your words just as surely as if they can smell it on your breath. Overlook a critical update, a zero-day exploit, and you could bring others down with you if money is changing hands. They want to avoid this. So in turn, they'll avoid you if they detect you're not practicing good security and there are ways to detect this without being too obvious.

That's the bad news. The good news is that it's 100% preventable if you practice good opsec, and where money is concerned, you want the best possible opsec money can buy.

Which brings us to *darknet markets*.

The number of such marketplaces on the deep web are numerous, and the risk of getting scammed is quite high. They also tend to go down rather frequently. It's one reason why you may not have heard about this popular site or that popular site. They're taken down quickly by either a venomous reputation of bad opsec or a law enforcement bust. Sometimes they piss off the wrong people and then spammers ddos the site. But there are numerous places one can go if you're curious about what is sold by whom. One place is DeepDotWeb, at:

http://www.deepdotweb.com/dark-net-market-comparison-chart/

And when I say *sold*, what I mean is anything you want that cannot be gained through the usual channels.

You should know that safety nets are a rarity in darknet marketplaces. Safety nets? They laugh at the idea. In fact you're likely to get scammed at least a few times before finding a reputable dealer for whatever goods you seek. And it really doesn't matter what it is, either. If there's money to be made, a scammer and a fool will met and the fool is soon parted with his money.

Teleportation devices? Pets? Exotic trees? It's all the same that goes around. Whatever is in demand will attract unsavory types and not just on the buyer's end. Therefore you must research any darknet market with absolute, rock-solid opsec within Tor and outside of it, being careful to visit forums and check updated information to see if any sites have been flagged as suspicious or compromised.

If you really need top notch cloak and dagger opsec, I'd recommend the following:

- Always use PGP to communicate.

- Never store crypto-currency at any such marketplace.

- Assume a den of thieves unless proven otherwise by *them*. The responsibility is their own just as it is offline; to prove they are an honest business. If you open your own, keep this in mind: customers owe you nothing. You can only betray them once and if you do, they will never do business with you again.

Now for some examples of phishers and scammers and other con games because at the end of the day, by their fruits ye shall know them.

1.) **Silk Road 2.0** (e5wvymnx6bx5euvy...) Lots of scams with this one. Much like Facebook and Google emails, you can tell a fake sometimes by the address. Paste the first few letters into a shortcut next to the name. If it doesn't match, steer clear.

2.) **Green Notes Counter** (67yjqewxrd2ewbtp...)

They promised counterfeit money to their customers but refuse escrow. A dead giveaway.

3.) **iPhones for half off**: (iphoneavzhwkqmap...)

Now here is a prime example of a scam. Any website which sells electronic gadgets on the deep web is ripe for scamming customers. Whereas in the Far East you will get counterfeit phones with cheap, Chinese made parts that break within a month, on the Deep Web they will simply take your money and say adios. Actually, they won't even bother saying that.

Many new darknet vendors will arise out of **thin air**, with rare products that will encourage customers to say 'shut up and take my money!'... without doing any research on their name or previous sales. A real hit and run operation. Hit quick and fast and dirty. Seduce as many as they can before the herd catches on to the wolf in disguise. Many newcomers try to blow it off. They think, "It's only a little money." It's this line of thinking that fuels the scammer industry. A little money from a lot of Tor users goes a long way in encouraging other scammers to set up shop.

Something to note is that when you ask them why they don't offer escrow, they say "We think it is unreliable/suspicious/unstable" amid other bullish excuses. It's better to hold on to your small change than leave a trail to your treasure chest.

Don't neglect your research. Check the usual waterholes and forums and especially the dates of reviews they have. Notice any patterns? Are good reviews scattered over a long period of time or are they 'all of a sudden', similar to how some Amazon scammers do with paid reviews that glow?

Take a lesson from the movie "Heat", with Al Pacino and Robert de Niro. They know when it is time to walk away. In the middle of a nightly heist, Niro goes outside for a smoke and to look around for possible risks of being seen. He hears a distant cough. Now, this is middle of the night in an unpopulated part of the city that comes from just across the street - a parking lot full of what he originally believed were empty trailers. They weren't. And his gut check affirmed it. So he walked back into the bank and calls everything off.

The other thing to watch out for is time. Some fake sites will set a short ship time and count on you not bothering to see the sale as finalized before you can whistle Dixie. After finalization, you're screwed since the money is in their wallet before you can even mount a protest.

When it is Okay to FE (Finalize Early)

FE means 'Finalize Early'. It's use online can usually be found in black marketplaces like Silk Road and Sheep's Marketplace. It simply means that money in escrow is released before you receive your product. Every customer I've ever spoken with advises against this unless you've had great experience with that particular business.

However, quite a few vendors are now making it a *standard practice* to require payment up front before you have anything in your hands. On more than one marketplace forum, there's been heated exchange as to when this is proper and when it isn't. One person may ask, "Is this guy legit? What about this Chinese outfit over here? He seems shady," and others will say "A friend said this guy is okay but then I got ripped off!"

You get the idea.

Here's my take on the matter.

1.) It's okay when you are content with not getting what you paid for. This may seem shortsighted, but think how many gamblers go into a Las Vegas casino and never ask themselves "How much can I afford to lose?" The answer is, not many. Vegas wasn't built on the backs of losers, and some merchants don't favor escrow at all. The bottom line: Don't spend more than you can afford to lose. Look at it the way a gambler looks at making money by playing poker. This applies to many purchases across the board.

2.) It's okay when you are **guaranteed shipment**. There are FE scammers out there that'll give you an angelic smile and lie as they chat you. This makes depending solely on reviews unsafe. A guy running a darknet store can be the best merchant this side of Tatooine and yet you may wake up one day to find yourself robbed. He's split with a million Bitcoins and you're left not even holding a bag.

When it is NOT Okay to FE

- When losing your funds will result in you being evicted, or cause a relationship to be severed. You've probably heard of not going into business with family or friends. Well, I take it a step further: Never borrow money from friends, and especially not family unless you want said family to come after you with a double-bladed ax. It happens. If you get ripped off, you lose not only the cash but the respect and trustworthiness of your family and that's like a hurricane coming to wipe your whole house right off the earth. Trust me on this. A bad reputation spreads quicker than a forest fire in July. Word spreads. You don't pay your debts, expect hurricanes, tornadoes and twisters from people you never even borrowed money from (but who're friends with the one you did). What's that saying in Game of Thrones?

A Lannister always pays his debts.

My own motto: Better to never get them in the first place.

MultiSigna

MultiSigna sounds like something a lowly peon might need to pass from ship to ship on the Galactica.

While not exactly mandatory, it makes for interesting reading, and is something Tor users might want to know about if they wish to make purchases anonymously. In a nutshell, here's what it is and what it does and why you should consider looking into it:

Whenever you buy something using it, the seller deposits money (in this case, Bitcoins) in a multi-signature address. After this, the customer gets notification to make the transaction ($,€) to the seller's account.

Then after the seller relays to MultiSigna that the transaction was a success, MultiSigna creates a transaction from the multi-signature address that requires both buyer and seller so that it may be sent to the network. The buyer gets the Bitcoins and ends the sale. Done.

It's a little confusing to wrap your head around it, but like everything else it will get easier the more you implement it. The important thing to know is that MultiSigna only exists as a verifier & cosigner of the entire transaction. If there's disagreement between seller and buyer, **no exchange** occurs. Remember the scene in Wargames when two nuclear silo operators have to turn their keys simultaneously in order to launch? It's pretty similar to that scene.

MultiSigna will of course favor one or the other, but not both if they cannot mutually agree. The upside is that is if the market or purchaser or vendor loses a key, two out of three are still available. A single key cannot spend the money in 2/3 MultiSig address.

Is it safe? Is it secret?

I don't recommend enacting a million dollar exchange for a yacht, or even a thousand dollar one as they both carry extreme, unnecessary risk, but ultimately it's your call. Just remember that trust is always an issue on any kind of darknet be it on Tor or Freent, and you're generally safer making several transfers with a seller/buyer who has a good history of payment. In other words, reputation is everything.

To that end, there's a few trustworthy markets with excellent history of doing things properly and with a minimum of risk. Blackbank is one. Agora is another. Take a look at the Multi-Sig Escrow Onion page here with Tor:

http://u5z75duioy7kpwun.onion/wiki/index.php/Multi-Sig_Escrow

Security

Now then. You might be wondering what the effect would be if a hacker gained entry to the server. What mischief might he make? What chaos could he brew if he can mimic running a withdrawal in the same manner that the server does?

If a hacker were to gain access and attempt to withdraw money, a single-signature would be applied and passed to the second sig signer for co-signature. Then the security protocol would kick in where these policies would be enforced:

1.) Rate limits, where the rate of stolen funds slows down.

2.) Callbacks to the spender's server: The signing service would verify with the original spender that they initiated and intended to make the spend. The callback could go to a separated machine, which could only contain access to isolated approved withdrawal information.

3.) IP limiting: The signing service only signs transactions coming from a certain list of IPs, preventing the case where the hacker or insider stole the private key.

4.) Destination Whitelisting: Certain very high security wallets can be set such that the signing service will only accept if the destination is previously known. Any hacker would have to compromise both the original sending server as well as the signing service.

Let me repeat that MultiSigna are *never in possession* of your bitcoins. They use 2 of 3 signatures (seller, buyer & MultiSigma) to sign a transaction. Normal transactions are signed by the seller and then by the buyer.

Purchaser Steps for MultiSig Escrow

The following is a simplified way of purchasing that I personally like to follow:

1.) Deposit your Bitcoins. This part's obvious, but know that purchase ability is granted after only 6 confirmations.

2.) Make a private & public key (Brainwallet.org is a JavaScript Client-Side Bitcoin Address Generator)

3.) Buy the item, then input the public-key & a refund BTC address

4.) Retrieve purchased item

5.) Input the private key and close. Done.

Below is a list of exchanges that support Multisig:

Bitstamp - Multisig service: https://www.bitgo.com

Rock Trading - Multisig service: https://greenaddress.it

TeraExchange - Multisig service: https://www.bitgo.com

BitQuick - Multisig service: https://www.bitgo.com

There is also a rather large (some say monstrous) list located at the following link:

http://bitcoinx.io/exchanges

The Long Arm of the Law

You most likely have questions at this point, questions like how secure your funds are when someone else acts as the gatekeeper and holds most of the keys.

Can the law steal funds?

- Assuming you mean U.S. law, then the answer is no since the wallet doesn't contain the money. The Bitcoin blockchain prevents this. Hackers cannot steal it either since two private-keys are required and they will need to steal 2 out of the 3 private key holders. This isn't likely to occur.

What about safety in using the private key?

- Never irresponsibly use the private key from your Bitcoin wallet. Create a new one instead. Give it the same love you give your Truecrypt or DiskDecryptor master keys.

This sounds awfully risky. Won't I get caught?

Let me use an archaic example. Way back in 1999, a kid's toy called a Furby put out by Tiger Electronics took the toy industry by storm. It resembled a hamster or owl-like creature and was the 'must have' toy during the run up to the 2000 Christmas season. It sold millions. Then on January 13th, 1999, the NSA decided to ban them from entering anywhere near the NSA's property because they believed that, while they looked cute sitting on an agent's desk, they were capable of recording classified meetings and/or documents. The media got wind of it and the next thing they knew, it made headlines around the country.

Later, the owner of Tiger Electronics stated publicly that "Furby has absolutely no ability to do any recording whatsoever, and I would have gladly told the NSA this if I was asked from anyone from the spy agency."

But let's say for argument's sake that you wanted to sell them to NSA employees anyway, consequences be damned. How might you get caught? That is after all, what you should ask yourself: what happens in a worst-case scenario, and what can you do to prevent it.

Well, at the risk of disappointment, it's the usual risks that get people caught. In other words, nothing that can't be applied to a half million other scenarios. But here's a list of the usual mistakes people make in dealing contraband, which can be anything from Cuban cigars to our beloved Furby:

- Bar Bragging
- Dropping too much personal data to strangers (See Ross Ulbricht)
- Selling contraband to undercover law enforcement
- Snitches
- Committing crimes while under surveillance

- Managing an operation that grows by leaps and bounds (with loads of new hired guns making mistakes).

The question you have to ask yourself is: How far will the police go to catch you? The answer is pretty simple: As far as resources allow. If they want you badly enough but lack the funding, they'll ramp up the threat you present to the media and churches and synagogues and cold call everyone begging for money to catch you since who knows how much damage those nasty purple Furbies can inflict on our sacred intelligence agencies.

Now, obviously the NSA likely would never bother with Furbies. But the FBI might if it meant flexing muscle in the headlines. I've seen them pull some absolutely ridiculous things to grab a front page news story. Flashy headlines mean more funding, and as you know, more funding means higher salaries. Bigger guns are just a bonus, but if they can't get that, then they up the armor like police vans and military-style trucks that resemble tanks.

Case in point: In 2010, police in L.A. organized a phony sweepstakes scheme in order to lure in those with outstanding warrants. Not kidding. Only they didn't come up with the idea themselves. They stole it from The Simpsons. They sent close to a thousand fake letters under the name of a marketing group only to have a little over half a dozen show up at the Los Angeles Mirada Inn for their free prize: A BMW 238. Not a bad prize for just showing up.

Only the joke was on them. Their smiles melted upon hearing those four dirty words, "You're all under arrest!"

Okay, so it's technically five words.

The poor saps even brought ID to verify their identities and when all was said and done, they might as well have slapped on the cuffs themselves. If they're willing to go through all that trouble just for a few misdemeanor crimes, imagine what they, along with the NSA, will do with a group of Tor users selling Furbies!

Jesting aside, the point of all of this is that this is just an OFFLINE example of what they're capable of. Imagine what one department can do by lying to an ISP or search engine.

Threats of fines. Warrants. Bad publicity. Subpoenas of users. A bad reputation they're not likely to recover from. Police in Vegas in particular love to play dirty; dredging up old laws to ensure every member in that Ferby operation has the book thrown at him.

In 2013, a Secret Service Agent arrested several online by selling them fake IDs. The kicker? They were all charged under the RICO Act of 1970. Originally created to put away mobsters, it allows them to lasso entire groups and charge each individual as if he committed the same crime everyone else in the group did... no matter the role.

Translation: The courier gets the same treatment as the ringleader, as do the buyers. Individually, not much prison time in the grand scheme of things in 1970, but being charged as a GROUP? Twenty years minimum. Al Capone never saw such a hefty sentence.

The other point is that it simply doesn't matter to a prosecutor if you're operating system is encrypted and they can't get the data. All they need to prove is that you were part of the *enterprise* operation. That can be done outside of your shiny new Western Digital hard drive by subpoena to your ISP and a few other services you may have subscribed to.

I like to think of Darkcoin as Bitcoin's smarter brother, and smarter in this case usually means darker. The best part of course being that it is constantly evolving and can only get better for you, dear student of anonymity.

Like Bitcoin, they're a privacy-centric digital currency based on the Bitcoin design. It's a design that allows for anonymity as you make day-to-day purchases on just about anything so long as the digital store offers it. One downside to Bitcoin is that anyone can see who made a purchase by studying the public blockchain. What Darkcoin does though, is anonymize your transaction further by using *Master nodes* - a decentralized network of servers that throw out any requirement for third-parties: Parties that could scam you out of your coins.

Though few outlets use it for the time being, it's one of the quickest growing digital currencies out there, and with an economy breaching over twenty million it's only a matter of time before even better currencies evolve.

And that's not all. It's "Darksend" feature is quite fascinating--increasing privacy by compounding a typical transaction with *two* other users. Needless to say, this is immensely attractive to a lot of Tor users who require high anonymity, and not just your average Tor user either. Whistleblowers, journalists, underground political movements. The good guys, all in all, who often get lumped in with the bad guys. You know the kind.

Terrorists. Contract killers. Tax evaders. Fallout players with the child-killing perk.

To that, I often hear the same arguments against using it that I've heard with Freenet usage. Namely, that bad guys want to evade detection. Bad guys trade Darkcoins. You use Darkcoins. Therefore, you must be one very bad guy.

(Cue torches and jinxed cats catapulted over a moat)

Heroin dealers love to use cash yet you never hear news outlets screaming about cash-only users linking to such a crime. Besides, the most corrupt money launderers are the central banks. It's they that allow states to borrow from future citizens to pay *today's* debts. One need only look at the National Debt to realize this.

That's not to say Darkcoins are without issues, for if you look around you're bound to hear a few excellent questions raised. Questions like:

- What if these "Master nodes" eventually form centralization? What then?

- What if Darkcoin is abandoned by the creators once the price goes through the roof?

- Who is trustworthy enough to "audit" Darkcoin? We saw an audit with Truecrypt in 2013 which turned out to show no backdoors... except that the developers shut it down with a cryptic message saying Truecrypt was Not Secure Anymore.

These questions may never be answered. But that shouldn't stop us from forging a new frontier in anonymity services.

Using Darkcoin for Business

It's much harder to run a Hidden Tor Service than it is to open a business using Darkcoin. It's so simple really that it almost boggles the mind what might be available in the future, and all with minimal risk to you.

If this appeals to you, then get the <u>Darkcoin Wallet</u> at their website (darkcoin.io) This is used to send, receive, and store Darkcoins with the benefit of using Darksend for 100% anonymity. Most of your patrons will want you to have a wallet, so better to learn it early in the business rather than later.

Pick a Transaction Processor

Below are a few you can research to your liking. Not every processor will suit everyone just as every bank or credit union will not appeal to everyone. You must judge these yourself, weighing your needs with whatever risk your business entails. I've tried most of these and came away satisfied but like everything else with crypto currency, what works for me may not work for you.

AltAccept

Fees

Transaction: 0.25% + 0.0005 DRK; Withdrawal: 0.01 DRK

CoinPayments

Transaction: 0.50%; Withdrawal: Network transaction fee (TX)

CointoPay

Transactions: 0% (coin to coin) 0.5% (coin to fiat); Withdrawal: Network transaction fee (TX)

Transaction: 0.5%; Withdrawal: Included with transaction fee

Some promo-graphics for your site, or whatever else you're using to advertise to your customers--you want them to know you accept Darkcoins, right?

Darkcoin Graphics (courtesy of the Darkcoin homepage)

After this you should signup to the Merchant Directory.

Then (optionally), do some reading on InstantX: https://www.darkcoin.io/wp-content/uploads/2014/09/InstantTX.pdf.

InstantX is a double spend proof instant transaction method via the masternode network. Not exactly light reading, but the more you know...

Further thoughts

No single entity has control of the entire system. Though the chance of an accident borders on the *not bloody likely*, you need to remember that Darkcoin is still in development and because of that, unforeseen things happen. So a healthy dose of due diligence is required. I suggest only purchasing with money that doesn't break the bank in case bad luck happens upon you.

Frequent backups are mandatory for your wallet, more than Bitcoin since the anonymizing process executes more transactions in the background. If you've ever used Freenet, you know how slow the network can be and how much of a system resource hog anonymity often requires. Thus, make a new backup of your wallet whenever a you hit a coin ceiling.

Darknet OPSEC

"Three can keep a secret if two of them are dead..."

\- Ben Franklin

The above quote was a favorite of mine in elementary school. It was just as applicable then as it is now as it goes hand-in-hand with having a secure mindset. Opsec, in other words.

And boy how I loved spouting that line. When a few kids asked me where it came from, I lied and said it was from High Noon. Then more asked a month later. I lied again and said it was from a Dirty Harry movie. Soon I was caught and couldn't remember what I had told to whom. I was busted.

The kicker was that I never really knew the origin until years later. I just thought it was a cool thing to say whenever a friend begged me if it was okay to relay a secret to a third friend. Rumors kill friendships, I told him. Some rumors, I warned, if validated could easily land me or any one of us in hot water. Even my red-headed chem teacher, who I was immensely liked, was off limits. Luckily I knew when to keep my mouth shut.

Well in hindsight, I suppose I could have told the hot Van Halen-loving teacher that I liked her. But I digress.

The point is that silence isn't just golden, it's rarer than rare. More rare than pink diamonds and encased in the same gold that built Sauron's ring to rule Middle Earth. Keeping your mouth shut about Darknet markets is more important than any encryption scheme you use, passphrase you know, Freenet group key or anything related to your Bitcoin wallet. Knowledge is power.

No, strike that. Knowledge is *potential* power, and power in slippery hands can be **disastrous** not only for you but everyone connected to you. Playing the bar braggart is jolly fun after a few beers and may win you a few points with the guys, but it gets more people imprisoned over frivolous reasons than anything else I can think of.

And I've seen more than one friend go down in flames because they mentioned a darknet market to someone they thought they could trust. But then that friend told someone else he trusted, more than anyone in the world.

To that end, let me relay a story on silence.

We'll start by calling my friend Grady. Grady, who thought he knew the ropes of OPSEC so well that he was The Man to go to when you had a problem. The big mistake came when Grady told his girlfriend and spared no details of his darknet adventures across the globe - how he'd maintained underground contacts on several continents and even had contacts in some of the alphabet agencies known for taking on Al Queda. She wasn't sure which was made up on the spot or exaggerated, since he'd been caught in a few minor white lies.

But that's not the point. The point is, he made himself sound like Agent Smith and Neo all wrapped up in one body that was anything but Kung Fu. When he walked and talked, it was like listening to a cat meow in a rain of sunshine. A talking wet sock. After a while, his bragging became so noxious that you avoided the guy altogether.

The worst part was that he trusted her to keep his secrets secret. This wasn't just dumb. It was dumb on a grand, epic scale. Legendary. Considering her trade (phone sex operator), it'd be like expecting Eve to eat the forbidden fruit all by herself. And we know how *that* story ends. Misery truly loves company.

The next thing he knew he attracted the attention of the authorities in Hong Kong, one of which happened to be of relation to his girl. It was her father. The secret was safe enough he supposed, that is, until he refused to marry this hyper-critical hypergamy girlfriend, claiming he feared settling down would kill his dreams. Well it killed something alright: His freedom.

Lesson? You can't fix stupid, so why would you trust it?

While you needn't go totally dark about your darknet knowledge for all eternity, in real life conversations - Social Media outlets, Tinder, Skype, etc., *mum should always be the word*. Invoke radio silence where applicable or better yet, feign ignorance. If they show you proof, deny deny deny. Then buy them a beer and leave. If they still persist, consider warning them you're about to sever all connections to them. Friends come and go, but freedom is priceless.

How to Setup a Hidden Service on Tor

A benefit to using Tor is that it allows you to create hidden services that will mask your identity to other users. In fact, you can have a website that is untraceable to you personally, provided you've taken all security precautions to keep your system updated. Here's an example of an onion site only accessible by using Tor:

http://duskgytldkxiuqc6.onion/

Naturally, you can't access this with your Firefox browser without using the Tor Browser Bundle. Hence the "hidden" name. The onion extension, along with a thousand other things, makes the site unaccessible to the regular open net.

This chapter will give you the basics on what you need to set up your own Tor hidden service should you have need of one. It's not meant to be an all-inclusive guide that covers everything and the kitchen sink, but only to give you an idea of the technical know-how you need to possess.

Step One: Ensure Tor Works

First, follow the directions on installing Tor, securing it against exploits and security vulnerabilities. Windows directions can be found at the Tor homepage. Each operating system has it's own vulnerabilities, with Windows being the worst. I recommend you go with Linux after you've mastered the basics as it gives you more control over Tor and is far more resistant to attacks than Windows.

Now might be a good time to state the obvious, something you've probably realized by now:

No two counter-intelligence experts ever do the same thing the same way all the time.

Put another way, there's no red pill that makes it "All Clear." No cheat sheet of Magic Opsec Sauce that everyone can master if they only gulp it down during a rain dance. Believe me when I say I've tried. I tend to make the same mistakes I did in my twenties, one of which occurred in Organic Chemistry way back in undergraduate college. My professors told me. No, warned me: "You can't memorize every organic compound combination in Organic Chemistry. There's far too many combinations so don't even try."

Instead, I was instructed to memorize the *general principles*, and it is those general principles from which you can derive a solution to every problem that comes about - as long as you practice every day. Technology, and by extension anonymity, is like that. Your strengths won't be your neighbor's strengths. Your weaknesses will be different than his. You adapt as you go along and I can guarantee you your skills as a hobbyist will far exceed those working on the government dole.

Step Two: Installing Your Own Web Server

A local web server is the first thing you need to configure. It's a bit more involved than space here allows (without jacking the price) but if you don't know what a web server is, there is a simple guide here at WikiHow. Just search for apache server and you'll find it.

One thing though. You'll want to keep this local server separate from any other installations that you have to avoid cross-contamination. In fact, you don't want ANY links between your hidden server and your day-to-day computer usage outside Tor.

Further, your server must be set to disallow any data leaks that might give away your identity. So you must attach the server to **localhost** only. If you're selling Furbies to disgruntled NSA employees and don't want the boss to know, use a virtual machine (vmware.com) to prevent DNS and other data leaks, but **only** if you can access the physical host yourself. Professional web hosting services like the Cloud are a big no-no since it is stupid easy for the admin to snatch your encryption keys from RAM.

Go to http://localhost:8080/ via browser, since that's the port-number you entered at creation. Copy a text doc to the usual html-folder and ensure it copies successfully by logging into the webpage.

Configuration Time

Now comes the part where most people quit. Don't worry, it isn't hard. It's just that beginners see these numbers and think "Oh no... math! I remember what Ms. Needles did to me in that tutor session. Never again!" Then they throw the book out the window.

But that's not what you'll do... because you want to be better than The Man at this anonymity stuff, right?

First, set your hidden-service to link to your own web-server. You can use Notepad to open your "torrc" file within Tor directory and do a search for the following piece of code:

########### This section is just for location-hidden services ###

As you can see, the hidden services function of Tor is edited out by the "#" sign, where each row relates to a hidden service. HiddenServiceDir is the section that will house all data about your own hidden service. Within this will be the hostname.file. This is where your onion-url will be.

The "HiddenServicePort" allows you to set a decoy port for redirects to throw off any efforts at detecting you. So add these to your torrc file.

HiddenServiceDir
/Library/Tor/var/lib/tor/hidden_service/
    HiddenServicePort 80 127.0.0.1:8080

Next, alter the HiddenServiceDir to the real directory from which Tor runs.

For Windows, use:
HiddenServiceDir
C:\Users\username\Documents\tor\hidden_service

HiddenServicePort 80 127.0.0.1:8080

For <u>Linux</u>:

/home/username/hidden_service/, substituting
"username" with whatever you named that directory.

Now then. Restart Tor after saving the Torrc-file
and it should be operational. Check your spelling if it
throws out any errors. Whenever I've encountered
any, that's almost always the culprit.

Next you'll see that two files are created: the
private_key and the hostname; private keys for your
hidden service which you should keep under lock and
key. The hostname is not your private key, however.
You can give this to *anyone* you wish.

A descriptor for the hidden service links to
other Tor servers and their respective directories so
that Tor users can download it anonymously when
they link or access to your hidden server.

Other opsec points of note

Some of these I've had to learn the hard way. Others come easy, but as we've seen, what's hard for me may not be hard for you.

- Visitors to your hidden service may be able to identify whether your web-server is Thttpd or Apache.

- If your offline 50% of the time, so then will your hidden service. Little bits (or lengthy ones, in this case) of data like this are useful to an adversary creating a profile on you. Be cautious.

- It is wiser to create a hidden service on Tor clients versus Tor relays as the relay uptime is visible to the public.

- Be aware that you are not a Node by default. On that point, it is advised to not have a relay running on the same machine as your hidden service as this opens security risks.

Shallot and Scallion Option

Just a quick mention here that I didn't find out about until many years of using Tor. You also have the option of using Shallot or Scallion (both at Github.com). Shallot allows one to create a customized .onion address for a hidden service, such as yyyyynewbietestyyyy.onion. This may prove useful if like me you want an absurd amount of control over things in Tor. Just be certain it doesn't correlate to anything in your 'real life'. More on that in a bit.

On Running a Hidden Tor Server (and other Opsec Magic Sauce)

Having used Tor for many years, it came as a pleasant surprise to learn how few incidents there were in which the NSA managed to disrupt Tor. And I don't mean spam, either, but rather something that brought large sections of the network to a grinding halt. As it turns out, they're bark is much worse than their bite, especially if one is vigilant with their own security setup.

The thing is, most Tor users couldn't be bothered. But then most users aren't interested in running a hidden server just as most P2P users don't bother seeding. Most are hit n' run downloaders. They know that as U.S. citizens they stand a good chance of getting sued just as a squirrel will get hoodwinked by a cat if he leaves his nuts out there long enough. So some users opt to not further their own security knowledge. Let the Tor devs do it, they say. Can't be bothered.

Except most of the Tor advice by Tor developers I've read come up woefully inadequate. In fact I find that, most of the time, they aren't paranoid *nearly enough*. It's always been my belief that you can never be sufficiently paranoid as far as protecting your freedom is concerned, since the powers that be want to capture it and bottle it the way a cancer captures control of a cell: One organelle at a time with little of it's environment aware of the slow attack vector. To be honest I suspect they *depend* on apathy and ignorance, to which many gladly oblige. Mr. Frog, meet boiling pot of water...

So then, what can we do and how can we do it? Well for starters, we can get the right security mindset which we discuss next.

Tor and Your PC

A secure computer is your best defense as the NSA mostly relies on man-in-the-middle attacks and browser exploits that deliver payloads to hidden Tor servers. That said, you should anticipate and **expect** such an exploit can infiltrate your system at some point. Things like Nits (network bugs), you have to be aware of. Thus the need to adhere to the following:

- Use Linux whenever possible. Yes, I know you're comfortable using Windows and think Linux can't run Planescape, but you won't if you're ISP is subpoenaed for something you said on the Ars Technica forum. So learn to use it.

The NSA typically targets the weakest system of an end user, or 'consumer' - you. To this, the Tor Browser Bundle for Windows was instrumental in taking down Freedom Hosting and Silk Road because of unpatched vulnerabilities. That, and a few rogue Tor exit nodes patched unsigned Windows packages to spread malware.

If you're new to Linux, I encourage to take a serious look at Linux Mint. If you're experienced, Debian is a good choice. Windows can't be trusted primarily because it is closed-source, but also because malware is more effective on it than Linux. If Linux is out of the question, consider Tails or Whonix as these apps come preconfigured to not allow any outgoing connections to clearnet.

Update Update Update!

Your PC must also be updated, always. Not updating leads to vulnerabilities and exploits such as those in Windows. Optimally you should ensure Tails is *always* updated each time you use Tor, and avoid any sites that use Java/Javascript/Flash or any kind of scripting as these execute code in ways you cannot see. Use these only in an emergency and never in your home system.

Personally, I try to avoid using cookies wherever possible. Consider installing the Self-Destructing Cookies add-on.

Lastly, if you're dealing in Furbies (or any illegal furry in your country) you should not use anything but a portable PC. Reason being is that your home PC is most likely not portable enough to be discarded in a trash can in the event of compromise.

Situation Awareness

Here we go again, preaching the same old song and dance. But reading things three times often becomes a trigger in the brain later on for taking action, so here it is, again, only said somewhat differently than in previous chapters - bearing in mind that situation security will be different for everyone.

If an agency can monitor your local connection as well as the link you are browsing, then (with sufficient resources) they can apply traffic analysis to pinpoint your real location. Therefore, I recommend you do not use Tor in your permanent residence.

Just to clarify, do not use Tor in your *legal* residence if doing any kind of covert work or anything *illegal* without strict security measures in place; the kind the average Tor user will likely overlook. Let that other guy learn his lesson. It's a tough break, but better him than you. He's a 19 year old named Jimmy who likes hacking into the Pentagon looking for UFO pictures. You're a 32 year old construction guy with two kids and a mortgage. Who has more to lose?

Right, you. So study counter-surveillance and counter-forensics like your life depends on it.

For enemies of the state-level operations, I would suggest not engaging anything even **near** your online PC at home, certainly nothing that makes you think you need Tor to hide it. It may be fine for private browsing but not for someone planning a coup, running an illegal operation (home bible study in Iran, for instance), or trying to disappear.

Be wary of using it in hotels as well, where often there are many cams watching with 24/hr surveillance. That location can be linked to Tor activity.

Do not use Tor more than a day in any specific location. A correlation-attack can be done in less than an hour if a black van is parked nearby--a van you will not see. They may not slap the cuffs on you as you walk out of the cafe that very week, but later they might. Consider the area a toxic dump after a day, regardless if you must travel to the next shop or town.

If you want to get really cloak and dagger about it, have an app running (an online multiplayer game, for instance, with paid alibis) while you're out and about doing your Tor activity that makes it look like you were home during that time.

"We've been watching you Mr. Anderson, and it seems you've been living *two* lives."
- Agent Smith, The Matrix

Darknet Personas

If you've read this far, then you're no stranger to Tor and probably have heard of at least one Tor bust where an undercover agent got a phone number or clearnet nic from someone they were targeting because the target trusted too much, too quickly. When it happens, it happens quickly. They more like lightning. Then months later his relatives find out in the news where he was all this time: in jail. No matter what country you reside in, you can avoid this by retraining yourself to be invisible. It's hard to do and sounds so much easier when Yoda says it, but there's no getting around it. You must *unlearn* what you've learned.

First, you must live and die by two personas, and consider every Tor session a property of your other self. The other guy. That shadowy thiefy looking taffer sitting in the corner. He's the *second* You, one that despises Incubus and loves Tool and views Neo as just another beta-orbiting punk who got the luck of the draw when Morpheus and crew unplugged him. This clone would never in a million years use Twitter or YouTube or any other traceable time wasters. He'd never hang out with you, nor would he call you up for a few Heineken beers in public. In fact, he hates beer and prefers J&B as he hacks with John Carpenter's The Thing OST playing as mood music in the background. That's the other *You*. The smarter you.

And he must be the new You **on Tor** and you must forever separate him from the non-Tor you.

His Facebook, Twitter and YouTube accounts are all fake, having never once used them on his home PC or even a nearby library. His nics are different, as is his passwords, likes/dislikes and even the fonts he uses to browse the Deep Web. Mixing this dark persona with your own would be like the boy made of matter kissing the anti-matter girl...

BOOM.

Further, any phone calls this person makes is done by prepaid phones that were not purchased by any credit cards he holds. Where electronics are concerned, he is a cash only guy and then only if he is twenty miles from home. Any *SIM* cards he uses are strictly used in conjunction with Tor activity and never used in phones the *other guy* uses. And he deliberately leaves false data trails wherever he goes. Kind of like the CIA does.

To better clarify this idea, let's assume John Doe doesn't know any better. Let's say he watches a movie on Netflix then does something stupid. He mosies on over to Freenet or some obscure Tor site and drops intel without even realizing it, all on account of his eagerness to share his great cinema experience with his darknet buds.

"Hey guys, just watched a cool flick with Russell Crowe. Kinda Michael Bay-ish and Liam Neeson's cameo was too short, but makes for a good flick if you want to learn how to disappear. But those police, sweet Jesus! Those rent-a-cop guys sure are as dumb as a sack of bricks!"

Police are dumb, he says.

Metadata is collected by Netflix just as it is with Google and Yahoo. Every single user. They know every film you viewed and even which ones you hated. He's even made forum posts indicating similar weather and, though not mentioning names, has griped about local politicians being handcuffed in very geographically specific arrests, even dropping the charges.

In light of the above, how many Netflix fans do you think watched this movie at the time of his Freenet or Tor post? How many in cities that had local politicians arrested for embezzling? How many with similar weather depicted in the film? Most likely less than ten. Maybe not even that.

There's also the handwriting element that'll give him away. Does he *mispell* the same words over and over? Throw commas like daggers? Misuse semi-colons and run-on sentences? System clock out of sync with his posts? All of this leads to a great profile that ties his IP address to his identity. Often it is enough to get a warrant if he so much as whispers that he's obtained any kind of contraband.

Unless of course, all of this info is tailor-made to fit the other *You*. We already know that the VPN called Hide-My-Ass as well as Hushmail and Lavabit stabbed their users in the back when threats by a judge became too heated ($5000 a day in Lavabit's case, until they forked over user data). And all this just so they could track Edward Snowden.

Bottom line: Learn from Snowden's mistakes. Take every company's claim of anonymity with a grain of salt. The proof is in the amount of arrests tied to said company or app. In the case of Freenet... none. But there's always a first time. Recall that they only have to get lucky once, which more often than not relies on your carelessness.

Tor Hidden Services - High Risk, High Reward

CNN along with FoxNews has been trumpeting the defeat of certain hidden services for a few years now. Services like Silk Road and Freedom Hosting, which if you listen to the media, signal the death of anonymity services. They're an easy target for the FBI since hidden services are not high on the list of priorities by Tor developers yet. Same for the NSA.

Both agencies know every trick and hack there is to know about running a hidden service. For this reason alone, so should you. This isn't to say you need the years of expertise to match their team of super hackers, but only that you need to be even more vigilant to run such a service than you do *visiting* such a service. When you run a hidden server on Tor, you are, as Ernest Borgnine so eloquently put it in Escape from New York, The Duke. A-number-one. If there is ever a leak sprung and you find your cards crumbling in front of you, then you only have yourself to blame.

Your number one priority is actually pretty simple. If you're the top dog, the administrator or the director of an operation, you must walk the walk yourself and be 100% self-sufficient. For Tor, that means the server must not be run under somebody else's control if you can help it, because if that service is compromised by your partner, you won't know it until it's too late unless you've worked out some rudimentary SOS signal - which is hard to do from a prison cell. In any case, *everyone* goes down if you misjudged. That means total anonymity, 100% of the time with world-class jewel-thief stealth ability - being able to predict with certainty when something's 'off' and when to pull the plug. This is especially true in countries that are hostile to democracy.

The Silk Road guys failed to exhibit much of this ability. In fact, looking through the court and FBI details regarding the arrest, one gets the impression he was very lax in basic security to say nothing about advanced OPSEC. He repeatedly made mistakes such that luck on the part of LE never really came into it at all. The guy was just sloppy.

The following bits of rules originally dealt with general spycraft, but were later honed to improve online anonymity. To that, they work quite well if you post it somewhere where you'll remember it. As well, each was only one sentence long. I've added my own gems to a few of them with the North Korea scenario as a base from which to grow your underground resistance, so to speak.

First Rule of Acquisition

Never, ever, ever run a hidden service within a Virtual Machine that is owned by a friend you barely know or a cloud space provider. Remember, all "The Cloud" is, is someone *else's* drive or network, and not your own. That means encryption keys can be dumped from RAM. And who owns the RAM?

Right. The cloudspace provider. If lightning should strike (and it will strike when you least expect it) there goes your anonymity as well as the anonymity of your visitors if they are lazy in their browser habits. The FBI delivered a payload this way to unpatched Tor Browser Bundles in 2013. If you own the machine outright, then it can be a different story.

But let's back up a few steps and assume you don't. How might you go about running it on a host system?

Well first off, you'd need two separate physical hosts from different parties, both running in virtual machines with a firewall-enabled operating system that only allows Tor network activity and *nothing else*. The second physical host is the one the hidden service runs from, also in a virtual machine. Secure connections are enabled by IPSec. If you don't recall what that is, it's actually pretty basic:

"IPSec is a protocol suite, for securing Internet Protocol (IP) communications by authenticating and encrypting each IP packet of a communication session. IPsec can be used in protecting data flows between a pair of hosts (host-to-host), between a pair of security gateways (network-to-network), or between a security gateway and a host (network-to-host)."

If an intruder agent tampers with anything, you will know about it and can shut down the service or move it to a safer place and all while still somewhat anonymous yourself. You can imagine how valuable this would be in North Korea.

If you were in that cesspool of a country, you would be more than a little paranoid if the server went down even for a few seconds. But you could always move it to a more secure location or even start over, and you may just want to since you wouldn't know if a RAID failure had occurred or if some commie jackboot was sending a copy of the VM to the higher ups.

Second

If going the host route, you must ensure that remote-console is always available to you by the host, any time you want. You must do everything remotely, in fact, and change passwords frequently via https. I'd say once per day as paranoia in such a climate as North Korea would be good for your health.

Third

You must never, not even once, access the service from home. Not from your Nexus 7. Not from your girlfriend's Galaxy Note. Not even via Tor from your backyard using your neighbor's WiFi. Using a VPN as well is risky unless accessed via secure location some distance away from your home base. It's overkill, I've heard some say for Canada and the

U.S., but then there is no such thing as overkill in a gulag. We've no idea where we'll be in twenty years, technologically or judicially.

Fourth

Move the service on occasion. Again, look at any Youtube video on how snipers train to take out an enemy. They move place to place after each shot to conceal the true location from the enemy. How often is up to you. Once a week? Once a month? I'd say every twenty-one days. You can never be too secure when running one of these, and luck always favors the prepared.

The Death of Anonymity

Prime minister David Cameron went on record in January, 2015 to say he wanted to outlaw all encryption-enabled messaging apps if the government cannot have backdoor keys to decrypt encryption. It's quite a preposterous idea, even now in 2015. While on the campaign trail, he said:

"Are we going to allow a means of communications which it simply isn't possible to read? My answer to that question is: No, we must not."

While he referred to mostly chat programs like WhatsApp and what not, you can bet the ranch he was also talking about apps like PGP, Freenet and the discontinued Truecrypt. Regrettably, he used the Hebdo (cartoonist) attack as justification.

Similar trends are evolving in Canada regarding VPN usage. New laws now require VPNs to identify customers who download copyrighted works like movies and games so that infringement notices get to the right person. And that's the problem. How soon that politicians forget how the internet actually *works*.

Implementing what they want means VPN providers must retain access logs for 6 months, minimum. This alone pretty much guarantees a VPN's ability to sell anonymity services (*privacy*, actually) will dissolve, thus leading to massive losses. Customers aren't stupid. They know when their privacy is being targeted.

They also know that VPNs assign shared IP addresses for customers. One might be yourself, all alone at night kicking back Rickard's Red while downloading the latest NiN video YouTube seemingly blocked, while the real bad guys get their way, every time.

The saddest part isn't that none of this won't stop terrorism or copyright infringement, or that it will hurt most private encryption vendors or that only politicians will have encryption while the citizens have none. No, the saddest part is that we'll have become the frog-in-the-pot who turns the oven on ourselves to full heat and then slip back into the pot. And all because someone more powerful than you said it was the right thing to do.

Our world will become a juxtaposition of opposites, where right is wrong and light is dark and no one has security except for the agents of the brave new world they'll build. Where to be more secure is to be *less* secure as us peons go, because if the government says so, well, that must be the gospel truth.

Because when's the last time a politician lied?

If you learn nothing else, remember two things: Backdoors are security holes in 100% of cases. The second one is similar: Anonymity and Privacy and the freedom that is born from it will only die **if we let it**.

Therefore we must be more vigilant than even the State, and more determined than our enemies if we're to hold onto the freedom we've earned by the blood of our patriots.

I wish you well and godspeed. May you be forever known by the strength of your enemies!

Closing Thoughts

As you can see, the powers that be are actively targeting your ability to make choices about your own freedom. They work in baby steps. A little here, a bill rammed through the legislature at midnight. They think you're stupid and blind as a bat. They think they can run your life better than you can. Only they can't.

Did the NSA stop the attack on Charlie Hebdo, the French cartoonist?

Did they stop 9/11?

The bombings in Spain?

A death from a thousand cuts, one at a time and before you know it you're feeling very light-headed but aren't sure why.

Just remember: Always take great pains to condition yourself to live by a strong *security mindset*.

That is, develop an ability to configure things logically and anticipate trouble way ahead of time, seeing weaknesses in your submarine before the water comes roaring in. Also known as a gut check. Better still is to have something set up long ahead of time. A plan B. A plan C. Even a plan D if you can afford it.

If there's one thing that you have that they don't, it's incentive. Incentive to work harder than they do. Incentive to strengthen your rights rather than weaken them. Incentive to forge allies of freedom and patriotism rather than allies of tyranny and darkness and rain and failure.

But most of them clock out at 5pm every day. Will you?

Want to Know More?

First off, I owe you a big thanks and a round of beer for downloading this book. You could have picked any one of dozens of great books on this topic. You took a chance with mine. So thank you for that. Seriously, reading to the end takes a strong mind. If you liked what you read then I need your help! Please take a moment to leave a review for this book on Amazon so others can learn to use Tor and Freenet and, well, protect themselves.

Speaking of *protection*, I've used a number of tools to get to where I'm at, and some of the topics that failed to pass the censors in *this* book quite miraculously managed to slip through in my *other* books. Go figure.

One thing though: when you have not one but two or three *silver bullets* to take down a werewolf, the better your chances of staying invisible to any other lycans roaming around out there. Mind you, I'm not prejudiced against those with Lycanthropy, as it is no laughing matter. But then neither is herd mentality.

So then. Don't use the same tools everyone else is using all the time. Mix it up a bit by checking out some other stuff of mine that did not see the light of day in this release:

More Kindle eBooks by Lance

Darknet: A Guide to Staying Anonymous Online (Audio & Kindle)
Invisibility Toolkit - 100 Ways to Disappear (Internationally)
Cell Anonymity: OPSEC for Android, Blackberry & iPhone
Anonymous File Sharing: How to Be a Ghost in the Machine
Social Media in an Anti-Social World
Tor and the Dark Art of Anonymity
Freenet: The Ultimate Deep Web Portal

Usenet and the Future of Anonymity